# taekwondo basics

# Taekwondo

## BASICS

### Scott Shaw

Photography by Hae Won Shin

TUTTLE PUBLISHING
Boston · Rutland,Vermont · Tokyo

First published in the United States in 2003 by Tuttle Publishing, an imprint of Periplus Editions (HK) Ltd., with editorial offices at 153 Milk Street, Boston, Massachusetts 02109.

Library of Congress Cataloging-in-Publication Data
Shaw, Scott, 1958-
   Taekwondo basics / Scott Shaw ; photography by Hae Won Shin
       p. cm.
   Includes bibliographical references.
   ISBN 0-8048-3484-9 (pbk.)
   1. Tae kwon do.  I. Title: Tae kwon do basics. II. Title
GV1114.9.S54 2003
796.815'3--dc21                   2003045819

Distributed by

**North America, Latin America, and Europe**
Tuttle Publishing
Distribution Center
Airport Industrial Park
364 Innovation Drive
North Clarendon, VT 05759-9436
Tel: (802) 773-8930
Fax: (802) 773-6993
Email: info@tuttlepublishing.com

**Asia Pacific**
Berkeley Books Pte. Ltd.
130 Joo Seng Road
#06-01/03 Olivine Building
Singapore 368357
Tel: (65) 6280-3320
Fax: (65) 6280-6290
Email: inquiries@periplus.com.sg

**Japan**
Tuttle Publishing
Yaekari Building, 3F
5-4-12 Osaki, Shinagawa-ku
Tokyo 141-0032
Tel: (03) 5437-0171
Fax: (03) 5437-0755
Email: tuttle-sales@gol.com

First edition
09 08 07 06 05 04 03  9 8 7 6 5 4 3 2 1
Printed in the United States of America

# table of contents

# Acknowledgments

Special thanks to Paul Crispell and Hae Won Shin for helping to demonstrate the techniques presented in this book.

# part 1
# introduction

**T**AEKWONDO, "the way of the fist and the foot," is the most practiced system of martial arts in the world. There are over fifty million practitioners spanning the globe.

When you mention the word "taekwondo," the first thought that comes to mind is often the image of a practitioner flying through the air and delivering a kick to his opponent. However, although taekwondo is known for its elaborate kicking arsenal, there is much more to this advanced system of martial arts.

At the root of taekwondo is an exact science of self-defense. Whereas many styles of martial arts utilize overexaggerated techniques, taekwondo has been continually refined and redeveloped to make all of its offensive and defensive methodology precisely direct. No unnecessary movement is utilized in taekwondo. Therefore, no energy is wasted. This is one reason that taekwondo has not only continued to gain loyal practitioners but has developed from a refined method of self-defense into an Olympic sport.

# chapter 1
# the history
# of taekwondo

THE FOUNDATIONS of taekwondo can be traced back thousands of years. Korea possesses a long and illustrious history of developing and refining advanced systems of martial arts. This history was idealized by the Hwa Rang warriors of the fifth century B.C. The "Flowering Youth," as they were known, brought an end to regional conflict, united the kingdoms on the Korean peninsula, and spread their understanding of Buddhism and warfare to the island nation of Japan. This historic transmission of knowledge helped to give birth to Japanese samurai culture. Although martial culture on the Korean peninsula dates back to the beginning of recorded time, the system of martial arts that came to be known as taekwondo is less than a century old.

## The Birth of Taekwondo

At the beginning of the twentieth century, Korea was occupied by Japan. This annexation was not lifted until Japan's defeat at the end of World War II.

With brutal Japanese occupation lifted, Korea went through a period of rapid cultural revival. During this process, the native martial arts, which had been banned by the occupying forces, experienced a renewal. The Korean people, swearing never to be overtaken by a foreign power again, embraced this spread of the martial arts throughout their nation. From this came the birth of the modern Korean martial arts.

Taekwondo has gone through a long process of evolution since its foundations began to be laid at the end of World War II. It took many years for the various Korean martial arts instructors to finally unite their individual *kwans*, or "schools," under the banner of taekwondo. To understand this process, we can look at the history of the modern Korean martial arts.

# The Kwans
## The Chung Do Kwan

The Chung Do Kwan was founded by Lee Won Kuk. (In Korean names, the surname, or family name, comes first, followed by given names. Thus, in Western usage, Lee Won Kuk would be "Mr. Lee.") This was the first school of martial arts to be established in modern Korea and was the first school to begin laying the foundations for what was to become taekwondo.

Lee Won Kuk began his career in the martial arts in 1926, at the age of nineteen, when he moved to Japan to attend college. During his time at the university he studied Shotokan karate directly from its founder, Gichin Funakoshi.

Lee eventually returned to Korea and began teaching karate in September of 1944. His school was located at the Yong Shin School in Seoul.

During the Japanese occupation, it was virtually impossible for a Korean to open a school of karate in his homeland. Due to Lee's close relationship with the Japanese governor general of Korea, however, he was one of the very few people who were allowed to do so. This led to widespread rumors and deep distrust of Lee. It was believed that he must be a Japanese sympathizer, or he

The Korean term *dojang* refers to a martial arts studio.

would not have been allowed to open his school. This distrust ran so deep that in 1945, when Korea was liberated, Lee was put on trial for his Japanese affiliations and had to temporarily close the doors of his school.

Lee was not convicted, however. Upon his acquittal, he became very proactive in his stance about Korean independence.

Lee formed a tight alliance with the Korean National Police. So much so, that when his Chung Do Kwan was reopened in Seoul, in April of 1946, it became known as the National Police Dojang.

The name *Chung Do Kwan* means "The School of the Blue Waves."

The first seventeen black belts of the Chung Do Kwan were:

Yoo Ung Jun

Son Duk Sung

Uhm Woon Kyu

Hyun Jong Myun

Min Woon Sik

Han In Sook

Jung Young Taek

Kang Suh Chong

Baek Joon Ki

Nam Tae Hi

Ko Jae Chun

Kwak Kuen Sik

Kim Suk Kyu

Han Cha Kyo

Jo Sung Il

Lee Sa Man

Rhee Jhoon Goo—
    the father of
    American taekwondo

In 1951, due to his age, Lee Won Kuk asked one of his senior students, Son Duk Sung to take over as the chief instructor of the studio. Son Duk Sung accepted this offer and thereby became the second grandmaster of the Chung Do Kwan.

Many of the Korean schools of martial arts closed their doors during the Korean War, and the Chung Do Kwan was no exception. It did not reopen until 1953. By this point, however, Lee Won Kuk rarely visited the school because of his advanced age. Son Duk Sung and the instructors Son had personally trained became the primary teachers of the kwan. As time progressed, several advanced students of the Chung Do Kwan branched off and founded their own kwans.

### The Chosun Yun Moo Kwan — Ji Do Kwan

The evolution of *chosun yun moo kwan* began in 1931 when Lee Kyung Suk, a Korean who taught judo, was allowed to establish the Chosun Yun Moo Kwan school in Seoul. He successfully operated this school of judo for several decades.

At the end of World War II, Lee Kyung Suk asked Chun Sang Sup to set up a course of *kwon bop* at his school. This program was named Chosun Yun Moo Kwan Kwon Bup Bu.

Chun Sang Sup began his martial arts training in judo while in high school. He then moved to Japan to attend Dong Yang Chuck Sik College. It was during this period that he was exposed to Shotokan karate, and he is believed to have earned a black belt.

Upon returning to Korea, Chun is believed to have secretly taught Shotokan

Kwon bop is one of the Korean terms used for Japanese karate.

The kwans founded by advanced students include:

1. Kuk Mu Kwan, founded by Kang Suh Chong

2. Jung Do Kwan, founded by Lee Yong Woo

3. Chung Ryong Kwan, founded by Ko Jae Chun

4. Oh Do Kwan, founded by Choi Hong Hi and Nam Tae Hi

karate to private students, beginning in approximately 1940. Because privately teaching karate was outlawed by the Japanese occupying forces, his teaching was not formally recorded until he established his training method after World War II.

Chun Sang Sup enlisted the help of Yoon Byung In to teach karate at the Chosun Yun Moo Kwan. Yoon was a fourth-degree black belt in Shotokan karate.

Yoon Byung In taught at the Chosun Yun Moo Kwan for approximately one year before breaking away and forming his own school, known as the Chang Moo Kwan. Chun Sang Sup again returned to full-time teaching responsibilities.

Chun's instruction continued until an evil twist of fate found him kidnapped and imprisoned by the North Korean military during the Korean War. He was never heard from again and was eventually believed to be dead.

Upon the loss of Chun, Chosun Yun Moo Kwan Kwon Bup Bu teaching passed to the hands of Yoon Kwe Byung, one of Chun's senior students. He renamed the school Ji Do Kwan, "Wisdom Way School."

During the 1950s, when the various kwans of the Korean martial arts began attempting to merge under one banner, Yoon Kwe Byung was against unification. Yoon wanted the Ji Do Kwan to remain free from organizational control, but the other senior members of the Ji Do Kwan disagreed. As a result, Yoon was ousted from his presidency, and Lee Chong Woo was elected the new president of the Ji Do Kwan.

Lee Chong Woo forged the Ji Do Kwan into one of the leading schools of martial arts in modern Korea. Its practitioners were noted for their consecutive wins at South Korean tournaments. Lee

The first ten black belts of the Ji Do Kwan were:

1. Bae Young Ki

2. Lee Chong Woo

3. Kim Bok Nam

4. Park Hyun Jung

5. Lee Soo Jin

6. Jung Jin Young

7. Lee Kyo Yoon

8. Lee Byung Ro

9. Hong Chang Jin

10. Park Young Kuen

The presidents of the Ji Do Kwan:

Founder and first grand master: Chun Sang Sub

Second president: Yoon Kwye Byung

Third president: Lee Chong Woo

Fourth president: Bae Young Ki

Fifth president: Lee Chong Woo

Sixth president: Lee Sueng Wan

also went on to hold several pivotal positions within the Korea Taekwondo Association and the World Taekwondo Federation.

## The Moo Duk Kwan

There are two distinct divisions of Moo Duk Kwan, both of which evolved from a single source in modern Korea. The first is most commonly known as *Tang Soo Do*. The second is the Moo Duk Kwan division of taekwondo. To understand how these two separate governing bodies came into existence, we must first view the birth of this system of self-defense.

The founder of Tang Soo Do Moo Duk Kwan was Hwang Kee. Hwang was an expatriate of Korea during much of its Japanese occupation. He details that he first secretly studied the Korean arts of *soo bak do* and *tae kyon* in his homeland, before leaving Korea in 1936 to work for the Southern Manchuria Railroad in China.

*Moo Duk Kwan can be translated as "The School of Military Virtue."*

In early interviews, Hwang Kee stated that he studied numerous systems of Chinese martial arts while living in China. Later, it was revealed that he had also studied a system of karate while he was there. Is it significant that this was revealed later—or it is at least notable.

Hwang returned to Korea near the end of Japanese occupation and formalized his system of self-defense on his birthday, November 9, 1945. In 1946 his system began to be taught at the Yong San Railway Station in Seoul. It was called *Tang Soo Do Bu*, and he titled his martial arts organization *Kyo Tong Bu Woo Hae*. The Korean term *tang soo* literally translates as "knife hand," and the Japanese character used to depict this term is the same one used for karate.

Since Hwang Kee's first school was in a railway station, many of his first

The first president of the Tang Soo Do Moo Duk Kwan was Hwang Kee. The first four presidents of the Taekwondo Moo Duk Kwan were:

1. Lee Kang Ik
2. Hong Chong Soo
3. Kim In Sook
4. Choi Nam Do

students were railway employees. The school flourished for many years. Then, like most schools of martial arts on the Korean peninsula, it was closed on June 25, 1950, at the onset of the Korean War.

In 1953, when the school reopened, Hwang Kee had changed the name of the system to *moo duk kwan*. He also changed the name of his organization to the Korea Soo Bahk Do Association. By 1955 this organization had ten gymnasiums, but its central headquarters remained near Seoul Station. During this same year, the Korea Soo Bahk Do Association hosted its first Sino-Korean martial arts championship.

By 1965, the various kwans of the modern Korean martial arts were merging under the banner of taekwondo. Hwang Kee resisted this trend, wishing to maintain control over his organization. As a result, two of his advanced students—Im Young Tek and Hong Chong Soo—broke away from their teacher, formed their own branch of moo duk kwan, and became a part of the Korea Taekwondo Association. From this act, two distinct systems of self-defense, both called moo duk kwan, emerged.

Many advanced practitioners of tang soo do moo duk kwan followed this lead and broke away from Hwang Kee. They each became part of the taekwondo branch of moo duk kwan.

Although the two moo duk kwans are relatively similar in style and structure, and most Korean moo duk kwan masters draw their lineage from Hwang Kee, the two moo duk kwans possess different forms and a somewhat different focus. The taekwondo branch of moo duk kwan does, however, possess substantially more members—approximately 500,000.

One interesting note is that tang soo do, unlike the other Korean martial arts, does not

The first blue belts of Tang Soo Do were:

1. Kim Woon Chang
2. Hong Chong Soo
3. Choi Hui Suk
4. Yoo Kwa Young
5. Nam Sam Hyun
6. Kim In Suk
7. Lee Bok Sung
8. Hwang Jin Tae
9. Won Yong Bup
10. Chung Chang Young

use the traditional black belt in its ranking system. Hwang Kee believed that black is the color in which all other colors merge—that is, any color that is mixed with black also becomes black. If an individual wears a black belt, it means that he has mastered the art. However, no one can ever truly master the martial arts, because they are a continual learning process. Therefore, advanced tang soo do practitioners wear a navy blue belt.

The early Chang Moo Kwan black belts were:

1. Lee Nam Suk
2. Kim Sun Gu
3. Hong Jung Pyo
4. Park Chul Hee
5. Park Ki Tae
6. Kim Ju Gap
7. Song Suk Joo
8. Lee Joo Ho
9. Kim Soon Bae

## The Chang Moo Kwan

The *Chang Moo Kwan* was founded at the YMCA in the Jong Ro section of Seoul in 1946 by Yoon Byung In. In Japanese-occupied Korea, Yoon is said to have studied a Chinese system of self-defense known as *joo an pa*. This system is more commonly known as *chuan fa*. He then moved to Japan to attend Nihon University. While there, he studied karate under the direction of Toyama Kanken, the founder of Shotokan karate.

When Korea gained independence, Yoon returned to his homeland and taught karate at the Chosun Yun Moo Kwan Kwon Bup Bu for approximately one year. He broke away from this school, and in 1946 opened the YMCA Kwon Bup Bu or Chang Moo Kwan. This school initially had over 500 students, but Yoon's training method was so severe that fewer than 200 students remained after only a few months.

In 1946 Lee Nam Suk was named the first official instructor of the Chang Moo Kwan. When Yoon Byung In went missing in action during the Korean War, it was Lee Nam Suk and Kim Soon Bae, another advanced student of Yoon's, who reopened the school at the Seoul YMCA at the end of the war.

## The Kang Duk Won

As the second incarnation of the Chang Moo Kwan came into existence in 1953, Lee Nam Suk and Kim Soon Bae began to have conflicts with two other senior students: Hong Jung Pyo and Park Chul Hee. These two men left and formed the *Kang Duk Won*, "House of Teaching Generosity," in the nearby Shin Sul Dong district of Seoul in 1956.

## The Song Moo Kwan

The *Song Moo Kwan* was founded in Kae Sung City, Kyung Ki Province, Korea, by Ro Byung Jick, on March 11, 1944. Like the Chung Do Kwan, this school was actually established prior to the end of Japanese occupation. The original classes of the kwan were taught at the Kwan Duk Jung School of Archery.

The name *Song Moo Kwan* means "The Ever-Youthful House of Martial Arts Training."

Due to the repressive political conditions, the kwan was forced to close its doors a few months later. It was not until May 2, 1946, that Ro could reopen his school in Dong Hung Dong, Kae Sung City, Korea.

On June 25, 1950, the Song Moo Kwan again closed its doors, due to the onset of the Korean War. On September 20, 1953, the school was reestablished in the Ah Hyung Dong, Mapo Gu district of Seoul.

The first black belts of Kang Duk Kwan were:

1. Lee Kum Hong, who would eventually hold the position of World Taekwondo Federation general secretary

2. Kim Yong Chae, who became the fifth president of the Korea Taekwondo Association

3. Lee Jung Hoo

4. Lee Kang Hwi

5. Han Jung Il

6. Kim Pyung Soo

7. Ji Seung Won

8. Im Bok Jin

Ro's training in the martial arts began in 1936 in Japan. He studied Shotokan karate alongside Chung Do Kwan founder Lee Won Kuk, under Shotokan karate's founder, Gichin Funakoshi.

## The Oh Do Kwan

The *Oh Do Kwan* was founded by General Choi Hong Hi and Major Nam Tae Hi. Both of these men were advanced military officers in the newly formed army of liberated Korea. Their classes were originally taught at the Korean Third Army Base, Yong Dae Ri, Korea.

Choi Hong Hi was born into a prominent Korean family. He moved to Japan in his adolescence to further his education. While there, he studied Shotokan karate and earned a black belt. At the point when

The first five Oh Do Kwan black belts were:

1. Nam Tae Hi
2. Baek Joon Ki
3. Choi Dong Hee
4. Kim Suk Kyu
5. Ko Jae Chun

World War II broke out, he was forced into the service of the Japanese military. After World War II and the defeat of the Japanese occupying forces, he became a pivotal figure in the newly formed Korean military.

Nam Tae Hi became a student of Chung Do Kwan immediately after Korean independence. He quickly mastered the art and began teaching at the Korean Army Military Signal School in 1947. During the same period, Nam Tae Hi met Choi Hong Hi. This laid the foundation for the birth of the Oh Do Kwan.

As the years progressed, in no small part due to General Choi's senior position in the Korean military, Oh Do Kwan became the main martial art taught to the Korean Army.

Many individuals already possessed a black belt by the time they were inducted into the Korean armed forces, but due to General Choi's influence, the rank of black belt was only accepted and transferable from students of the Oh Do Kwan and the Chung Do Kwan. Those practitioners who held black belts from other kwans had to be retrained and retested to be considered for official black-belt status. This regulation was questioned by many practitioners of the modern Korean martial arts, but it was, nonetheless, the impetus that brought the various schools of the Korean martial arts together under the banner of taekwondo.

## The Unification of the Kwans

The unification of the Korean kwans, congregating under one banner, began in the early 1950s. This began when the leaders of the various schools first began to come together and attempt to form a central governing body. Due to the outbreak of the Korean War, however, these initial attempts did not prove to be successful.

### The Korea Kong Soo Do Association

During this period of war, several kwan leaders, who were living in the Korean wartime capital of Pusan, formed an alliance and vowed to create a governing body. At the end of the Korean War, the kwan leaders joined forces and set about formalizing an organization. They named this governing body the Korea Kong Soo Do Association.

Because politics influenced all aspects of Korean culture, the first president of the organization was Jo Young Joo, the head of the Association of Korean Residents in Japan. He was soon followed by a new president, the Republic of Korea minister of finance, Lee Joong Jae. Ro Byung Jick was elected its director and Lee Chong Woo the secretary general.

The focus of this organization was to provide a standardized system of testing. As each kwan leader had his own system of teaching and testing, this proved to be problematic. Nonetheless, the first two tests were given at the central dojang of the Chung Do Kwan, which was actually located in the Si Chun Church, when it was not in use for worship. The next two tests were given at the Chae Shin Bu Dojang.

The term *Kong Soo Do* was adopted because this term was commonly used to describe kwon bop, "karate," in the Korean language.

At this time, the rank of fourth dan was the highest degree awarded by the Korea Kong Soo Do Association. This rank was given to the original kwan founders and the advanced teachers of the various kwans.

There was immediate conflict among some founders of the original Korean kwans, however. They were dissatisfied with the promotion standards within this organization. Two of the leaders of this dispute were Hwang Kee (Moo Duk Kwan) and Son Duk Sung (Chung Do Kwan).

Hwang Kee was the first to leave the organization, one month after it was formalized. His departure was in no small part due to the fact that he was not given a position on the Central Testing Committee—which set the standards for the organization. Approximately one month later, Son Duk Sung removed his group, Chung Do Kwan, from the organization for the same reason.

It was less than a year before the Korea Kong Soo Do Association began to disintegrate. Hwang Kee was pushing forward his Korea Tang Soo Do Moo Duk Kwan Association, by petitioning the Korea Amateur Sports Association to grant it formalized status. This attempt eventually failed because it was blocked by a key player in the Korea Kong Soo Do Association, Ro Byung Jick. What this

The first black belts of the Song Moo Kwan were:

1. Lee Hwa Soon
2. Lee Young Sup
3. Kim Hong Bin
4. Han Sang Min
5. Song Tae Hak
6. Lee Hwi Jin
7. Jo Kyu Chang
8. Hong Young Chang
9. Kang Won Sik

attempt did, however, was to fuel the independence movement among the other kwans that had not become formalized within this group. Some of the kwans that desired ongoing independence were the Han Moo Kwan, the Jung Do Kwan, and the Oh Do Kwan, all of which continued to hold their own promotional testing.

It was particularly the Oh Do Kwan that eventually caused the Korea Kong Soo Do Association to fail, primarily because of the influence General Choi's Oh Do Kwan had with the Korean military and with the Korean government. Without General Choi's support, a successful central association was virtually impossible.

## The Korea Taekwondo Association

In 1959 General Choi petitioned the Ministry of Education and the Korea Amateur Sports Association to found a new organization. Due to his close ties to then Korean president Rhee Seung Man, the acceptance of this organization was virtually ensured.

General Choi coined the name taekwondo. He established it in the minds of the Korean public by having military and civilian students of the art yell, "Tae Kwon," each time they executed a technique. There were several names being considered, and extensive debates went on. The six primary kwans—the Chung Do Kwan, Oh Do Kwan, Song Moo Kwan, Chang Moo Kwan, Ji Do Kwan, and Moo Duk Kwan—came together, and the name taekwondo was finally accepted as the title for the unified style of the Korean martial arts. This acceptance was attributed to the fact that it closely resembled the name of the ancient Korean martial art, tae kyon.

In 1959 the affiliated Korean kwans finally became formalized as The Korea Taekwondo Association. General Choi Hong Hi was elected its president. Ro Byung Jick of the Song Moo Kwan and Yoon Kwe Byung of the Ji Do Kwan were elected the vice presidents. Hwang Kee of the Moo Duk Kwan was appointed the chief director. Hwang Kee's participation in this organization was short-lived, however. He broke away from the group the same year.

On May 16, 1961, South Korean president Rhee Sang Man was overthrown by a military coup d'état. South Korea entered into a period of internal chaos. The Korea Taekwondo Association collapsed.

### The Korea Tae Soo Do Association

During this period of internal disruption and military rule, the kwans were forced to organize into one body by Governmental Decree #6, which ordered all schools of the Korean martial arts to unify under one banner. As a result, the leaders of the kwans again came together and attempted to form one organization. Heated debate went on throughout 1961. The group emerged with the name Korea Tae Soo Do Association.

As was the case with the Korea Kong Soo Do Association, the primary concern was formalized teaching and promotion standards. To help to achieve this, an inspection team was set up and deployed to the various kwans in order to enforce the use of standardized *hyung* (forms) and *taeryun* (free-sparring techniques).

Although the Korea Tae Soo Do Association was the governing body that laid the foundation for taekwondo, there was still a large amount of infighting. Many of the advanced members did not like the fact that they were being told what they must teach and how they must promote their students. Again, at the forefront of this controversy was Hwang Kee. On July 20, 1962, Hwang Kee wrote his letter of resignation from the organization.

### General Choi and the Korea Tae Soo Do Association

Although General Choi was instrumental in the coup, it is important to note that his previous close association with ousted President Rhee prevented him from playing an important role in the formation of this organization. In fact, although he once held the pivotal positions of commander of the Sixth Korean Army and director of intelligence, he was extremely disliked by the new Korean president, Park Chung Hee; General Choi had once been President Park's superior officer. As a result, Choi was forced to resign from the military and was sent to Malaysia in the capacity of ambassador.

The Korea Tae Soo Do Association remained without a president for approximately one year after it was founded. Finally, General Choi Myung Shin became its first president on December 28, 1962.

During this same period, Hwang Kee was granted governmental recognition for his organization by the Korea Amateur Sports Association and the

Ministry of Education. This action allowed his Korea Soo Bahk Do Association to remain free from interference throughout the years ahead.

*Taekwondo was given its name by General Choi Hong Hi in 1959.*

## The International Taekwondo Federation

In 1965 General Choi Hong Hi returned from Malaysia to South Korea. Soon after that, he was elected president of the Korea Tae Soo Do Association. He called together the General Assembly and proposed a vote to change the name of the organization back to the Korea Taekwondo Association. The name won by one vote.

By 1966 General Choi had formed the International Taekwondo Federation to help taekwondo spread across the globe. In that same year, due to many internal political factors, he left South Korea, moving himself and the headquarters of the International Taekwondo Federation to Canada.

## The World Taekwondo Federation

Deputy director of the Republic of Korea Presidential Protective Forces, Dr. Kim Un Yong, was elected the president of the Korea Taekwondo Association on January 23, 1971. Although he initially declined the position due to the continued conflicts within the organization, he was asked by the Korean government to accept and to cleanse the association. This he accomplished with great success.

Believing that taekwondo was a Korean martial art and its governing body should be based in Korea, Dr. Kim dissolved the relationship between the Korea Taekwondo Association and the International Taekwondo Federation.

In 1973 the World Taekwondo Federation was formed, and Dr. Kim was elected its president. This organization has led the martial art of taekwondo into its status as an Olympic sport.

# chapter 2
## the philosophy
## of taekwondo

**M**OST SYSTEMS OF MARTIAL ARTS promote the philosophy that practitioners should constantly be aware of their environment and be at one with nature. The philosophy of taekwondo is designed to teach practitioners to raise their body and mind to a new level of physical and mental awareness. These abstract concepts are lost to the minds of most modern practitioners of the martial arts.

The philosophy of taekwondo, however, is rooted in reality. First, it trains the body of the practitioner. The mind then naturally falls into place. Through taekwondo's refined physical training, the practitioner is no longer dominated by the fears that plague modern society—such as being accosted on a dark street corner or being overpowered by a bully. From the knowledge that one can protect oneself comes the experience of assuredness. Those who are self-assured are not swayed by the need to prove that they are better and stronger than others, or that they can overpower someone else. Instead, the taekwondo practitioner can embrace self-confidence without the need for conflict or confrontation. From this arises a oneness of body and mind, which causes the

Taekwondo develops self-confidence and oneness of body and mind, which leads to the physical harmony that is at the goal of taekwondo training.

taekwondo practitioner to enter a state of physical harmony. As time progresses, this harmony is projected from the individual, thereby making the world a better place.

# chapter 3

# the branches
# of taekwondo

## WTF and ITF

**T**HERE ARE TWO primary branches for the art of taekwondo. They are: The World Taekwondo Federation (WTF), head-quartered at Kukkiwon in Seoul, South Korea, and the International Taekwondo Federation (ITF), originally based in Canada. Of these two, the WTF possesses substantially more members.

There are two primary organizations that have guided the evolution of taekwondo: the World Taekwondo Federation (WTF) and the International Taekwondo Federation (ITF).

## The Differences and Similarities

The differences between these two primary branches of taekwondo principally involve their emphasis on self-defense. Whereas ITF taekwondo has kept its primary focus upon self-defense, with competition as its secondary concentration, WTF taekwondo has come to place its primary emphasis upon competition. WTF taekwondo has caused many of the traditional taekwondo techniques to be streamlined, refined, and focused upon a minimum of movement. This is not to imply that the WTF student does not learn self-defense, however, because what a student actually learns in the various schools affiliated with one of these governing bodies is largely determined by the instructor.

These two institutions prescribe different sets of forms for their students to practice. However, although these differ in defensive and offensive implementation, they both utilize the same style of techniques. The language of the two groups is also somewhat different. The various fighting techniques are oftentimes referred to by different Korean terminology. The essence of these techniques remains the same, however.

Ultimately, there are more similarities than differences between these two primary branches of taekwondo. The techniques they teach are based upon the same fundamental understanding of self-defense, and the martial philosophy is very much the same.

Although the WTF and ITF are the two largest branches of taekwondo, there are an untold number of smaller organizations that exist to promote the art of taekwondo throughout the world. Of these, perhaps the most noteworthy are the original kwans.

## The Kwans

It was the hope of the Korea Taekwondo Association that all of the original Korean kwans would merge, drop their names, and move taekwondo forward under the guidance of one overseer organization. To some degree, this did occur. Most notably, the name "taekwondo" was accepted by all of the original kwans, and most kwans practice the same set of WTF preset training forms—now most commonly known by the Korean word *poomse*. What also occurred, however, was that virtually all of the original kwans held onto their names and continued to promote their own unique interpretation of taekwondo. They never wholly dissolved. In some cases, the original founder of the kwan is still alive. In other cases, the kwan is run by an elected president. Thus, the kwans are still very much in existence and continue to issue rank and instructor certification.

Virtually all of the remaining original Korean kwans are associated with the WTF. In some instances, a black-belt kwan member is certified by both the kwan and the WTF. More commonly, however, especially in the West, this is not the case. Rank certification comes solely from the kwan. As the WTF no longer recognizes kwan certification, certified kwan members must then go through additional testing at Kukkiwon if they wish to hold WTF rank or instructor certification.

The propagation of the kwans has also continued. Many taekwondo masters, originally certified by a kwan, have created organizations all around the world that bear the name of the original kwan but are no longer directly linked to it. These organizations commonly provide rank and instructor certification sanctioned solely by the individual association.

Virtually every country on earth has a tae-kwondo association. Examples include: the British Taekwondo Control Board (BTCB), the Egyptian Taekwondo Federation (ETF), the Hong Kong Taekwondo Association (HKTA), the Japan Taekwondo Federation (JTF), the Korea Taekwondo Association (KTA), and the United States Taekwondo Union (USTU).

# Affiliate Organizations

Under the umbrellas of the WTF and the ITF are smaller, affiliated organizations. These associations are based throughout the world and were founded by advanced masters of taekwondo in order to promote the ongoing expansion of their parent organization. In most cases, these affiliate associations offer rank and instructor certification from both their own association and their parent organization. These groups are designed to provide a student or instructor with a direct link to one of the primary governing bodies.

# Olympic Taekwondo

The WTF is the sole source for taekwondo's inclusion in the Olympic Games. Therefore, the WTF has designated governing bodies that function to promote taekwondo as an Olympic sport. There are two levels of these groups. The first are the larger administrative bodies that oversee entire continents. They are the Africa Taekwondo Union (AFTU), the Asia Taekwondo Union (ATU), the European Taekwondo Union (ETU), and the Pan American Taekwondo Union (PATU). Under the direction of these associations are the national governing bodies that oversee Olympic-style taekwondo competitions and organize national teams.

To participate in any sanctioned Olympic-style event, a taekwondo practitioner must become a member of the organization in his or her country that has been established for this purpose.

# Independent Organizations

Many countries around the world have seen the rise of independent taekwondo organizations. These independent groups are commonly founded with the premise that their organizers do not wish their curriculum to be governed by an overseer association. As a result, the majority of these associations are not formally affiliated with either of the two primary governing bodies and are not formally associated with any of the original Korean kwans. Thus, all of their rank and instructor certifications are wholly organization-based.

In some cases, these independent associations have been founded by advanced masters of taekwondo who are certified by one of the two primary associations and perhaps one of the original kwans. In other cases, independent organizations have been founded by individuals trained in a more eclectic style of taekwondo that possesses little resemblance to the traditional art. Over the years, some independent organizations have become established and respected entities, while others lasted for a while and then dissolved.

# part 2
# getting started

**B**EGINNING TAEKWONDO training is no doubt the most difficult step to take in your immersion in the art. Although taekwondo schools can be found in every country across the globe, you must find the right school and the right instructor to meet your specific needs.

To provide you with an understanding of what you can expect as you walk through the doors of a dojang, this section will discuss some of the things you may encounter.

# chapter 4
# choosing
# the right school

**C**HOOSING THE RIGHT SCHOOL of taekwondo is essential if you are to maintain an ongoing interest in the art, while continuing to grow as a human being. Therefore, your enrollment in a school should never be taken lightly.

It is important to understand that what is right for one person is not necessarily right for another person. If somebody tells you that he or she attends the best taekwondo school on the planet, that does not mean it is the right studio for you.

Choosing a school of taekwondo must be done scientifically. You must study all of the elements of the school and then make a conscious decision about whether or not it is the right place for you to train.

## Ten Questions

The most important thing you can do before you choose a school of taekwondo is to go and watch a class at the studio you are considering attending. As you do, ask yourself these questions:

1. Is the school teaching what I want to learn?
2. Are the classes taught in a manner that will be beneficial to me?
3. Does the senior instructor teach the class, or does he have his students teach the class?
4. Are the beginning students treated with respect?
5. Are the white belts (beginners) at the school left to learn the techniques completely on their own, or are there advanced students helping them on their way?
6. How long has the school been in business?

7. Is the school affiliated with a large taekwondo governing body, or is it teaching an independent style?

8. Is the school's primary focus on self-defense or competition?

9. What are the belt promotion standards for the school (how long does it take to advance between belts, and what is the price of promotion)?

10. Do I have to sign a contract when I join the school, or are payments made on a month-to-month basis?

Always ask if it is a school's policy to offer a free trial class. Even if it is not, they may make an exception.

## The Hype

When you go to watch a class for the first time, you will probably be given the hard sell by the instructor or one of the senior members of the school. They will usually attempt to convince you that their school is the best in the area, and that all other schools are not up to their level of expertise. This is a very common practice, so it is essential that you do not allow yourself to be drawn into a school that you do not truly wish to attend.

Some schools allow you to take a free introductory class. This is an exceptional way to decide if a school is right for you. With a free class you get to actually experience a school's method of training.

## The Instructor

An obvious selling method in taekwondo is for an instructor to list all of his accomplishments. A taekwondo instructor's credentials are, obviously, an essential element in making your decision about where you will train. Accomplishments, however, do not necessarily mean that a particular taekwondo instructor is a dedicated teacher or the right instructor for you. Just because an instructor tells you that he is a "World Champion," "Ninth-Degree Black Belt," "Supreme Grand Master," or "Olympic Coach," don't assume that he is a competent instructor. When seeking out a school of taekwondo, you must weigh the instructor's accomplishments against his teaching ability.

It is essential to keep in mind that many taekwondo instructors have relocated from South Korea. Taekwondo training in South Korea is vastly different

You are the customer, so never be forced into signing a contract that you do not feel 100 percent comfortable with. If a school cares more about money than the student, it is probably not the right school for you.

from what one commonly experiences in the West. It is much more intense. For example, the average Western student would not appreciate being struck with a bamboo shaft when he performs a technique incorrectly. This, however, is a very common occurrence in the schools of taekwondo in South Korea. Some teachers bring this training method with them, so you must find a school where the instructor meets your specific training needs. The only way to do this is to observe the class.

## The Contract

Schools of taekwondo are martial arts businesses. In recent years it has become a common practice for schools to require new students to sign contracts. These contracts cover a prescribed period of time—anywhere from three months to three years.

Commonly, the longer you sign up for, the less your monthly payments. Although this sounds good, it does have a downside.

The student contracts presented at a martial arts studio normally specify that you must pay your monthly membership fee whether you attend classes or not. If you spend a few weeks at the school, discover that you hate it, and quit, you will still be responsible for paying the monthly fee until your contract has expired.

Ideally, before entering into any contract, you may want to sign up for a month to get a clear picture of what the school's training program actually entails and to see how much progress you make in that time. If the school management refuses to let you do this, it will give you a clearer idea of the school's motivation—money, as opposed to true taekwondo training.

**S**EVERAL FORMALITIES have been incorporated into the curriculum of taekwondo, to encourage students to express respect for the art, their school, their senior practitioners, and their teacher. The first thing one notices in a taekwondo class is the uniform.

## The Dobok

The dobok is the training uniform a taekwondo student wears during classes. It consists of loosely fitting pants, a loosely fitting top, and a belt.

The color white symbolizes purity and innocence, which is why beginners wear a white uniform.

The beginning student of taekwondo wears a white dobok. As the student of taekwondo is just beginning his journey through the art, he also wears a white belt with his dobok.

In South Korea, junior black belts do not wear the black belt. Instead, they wear a belt that is half red and half black, to signify their junior status.

The novice taekwondo student is taught from the very beginning that he must respect his dobok. He must keep it clean and fold it appropriately after training.

### Wearing the Dobok

Showing respect for the dobok demonstrates respect for the art of taekwondo, for one's school of taekwondo, and for one's instructor. For this reason, the taekwondo uniform should never be worn on the streets. A student should arrive at class with plenty of time to change from his normal street clothing into his dobok. By doing this, the student honors taekwondo by keeping this essential element of the art from inappropriate environmental exposure.

The dobok is designed to be the ideal garment to wear during taekwondo training, so the student is never allowed to make modifications to the uniform. Modifications even as trivial as rolling up the sleeves on a hot day are not allowed. It is understood that altering a dobok in any way expresses disrespect for taekwondo. Therefore, this is never done.

## The Taekwondo Belt System

Taekwondo practitioners wear different colored belts to symbolize the level of expertise they have achieved in the art. There are nine steps and five colored belts in the promotional system of taekwondo. The belts are: white, yellow, blue, red, and black. Although these are the formalized belt colors of taekwondo, some schools have added additional colors as a motivational tool for the students.

The colors of the belts are symbolic of taekwondo's philosophic basis. At the root of this idea are the beginning and ending belts: white and black.

### The Taekwondo Lower Belts

Ninth gup white belt

Eighth gup yellow belt

Seventh gup yellow belt

Sixth gup blue belt

Fifth gup blue belt

Fourth gup blue belt

Third gup red belt

Second gup red belt

First gup red belt

First dan black belt

The student of taekwondo begins training as a white belt. He progresses through the rank system from ninth *gup*, or "grade," to first gup. This descending manner of ranking symbolizes that the taekwondo student is ascending toward black-belt status.

The white belt and the black belt symbolize *um* and *yang*. This ancient philosophic concept is more commonly known as the Chinese principles *yin* and *yang*.

The concept of um and yang describes the interlinking diversity of this universe. White symbolizes day, while black symbolizes night. White represents lightness, as black represents fullness. White is purity, whereas black is knowledge, and so on.

It is understood in the philosophy of um and yang that one element cannot exist without its counterpart. Thus, the entire universe is based upon a system of duality. In terms of taekwondo, this represents the fact that the student learns from the instructor, while the instructor's function depends upon the student.

The three remaining belts have primary colors: yellow, blue, and red. These represent a student's progression from the realm of naiveté to the deeper dimensions of knowledge.

## Wearing the Taekwondo Belt

The taekwondo belt is tied in a very specific manner. It loops around the body two times and then is tied in front in a triangle-shape knot. The

*The conscious tying of the taekwondo belt alerts the student to be aware of what is known in Korean as the tanjun, the body's center of gravity. This is the bodily location where ki, or internal energy, is harnessed. This is a very sacred location on the body, as such it is treated with the highest respect.*

wearing of the belt and the tying of the knot, which binds it to your body, are symbolic gestures and should never be taken lightly. Tying your belt in this predetermined fashion represents that you are focusing your mind and your

The word *gup* is the Korean term used to describe grades 1–9 in taekwondo ranking. The word *dan* is used to describe the black-belt ranking. A *pum* is a junior black belt and a *Sabumnim* is a master of taekwondo.

body, organizing your thoughts, and readying yourself to enter into taekwondo training. The triangle-shape knot represents oneness of purpose.

## Understanding the Taekwondo Black Belt

Depending upon the school and the governing body, it can take anywhere from one and a half years to four years to earn a first *dan*, or "degree," black belt in taekwondo. One must be at least sixteen years old to obtain the taekwondo black belt; younger students who have studied taekwondo for the necessary amount of time and have demonstrated proficiency in the art are awarded the junior black belt. Whereas the adult taekwondo black-belt holder

# Taekwondo Black Belt Advancement

| Dan Level | Title | Requirements |
| --- | --- | --- |
| First dan | | Black Belt |
| Second dan | | Two years of continued training after receiving the first dan |
| Third dan | | Three years of continued training after receiving the second dan |
| Fourth dan | Instructor | Four years of continued training after receiving the third dan |
| Fifth dan | Master | Five years of continued training after receiving the fourth dan |
| Sixth dan | | Six years of continued training after receiving the fifth dan |
| Seventh dan | | Seven years of continued training after receiving the sixth dan, and the individual must also have made a substantial contribution to the art |
| Eighth dan | Grand Master | Eight years of continued training after receiving the seventh dan |
| Ninth dan | | Nine years of continued training after receiving the eighth dan |
| Tenth dan | | Founder of the system or president of an organization |

possesses a dan ranking, a junior black belt is referred to by the Korean term *pum*.

It is essential to understand that simply achieving a first dan black belt in taekwondo does not make one a master of the art. In fact, those who are awarded the first through third dan black-belt rankings are considered to be only advanced students of taekwondo. It is not until a taekwondo practitioner reaches the fourth dan level that he or she is considered an instructor. One is not considered a master of taekwondo, *Sabumnim*, until one reaches the fifth dan level.

# the taekwondo class

A TAEKWONDO CLASS is made up of eleven primary elements. Although the focus of each class will vary according to the instructor, these eleven elements will always be included in the overall curriculum of a school of taekwondo:

1. Bowing
2. Warmup
3. Blocking practice
4. Punching practice
5. Kicking practice
6. Forms practice
7. Self-defense training
8. One-step sparring
9. Three-step sparring
10. Sparring
11. Meditation

A taekwondo class begins when the students are called together by the instructor. The students line up in the appropriate location designated by the school. The senior students are always in front of the class. From there, the students fall into place in accordance with their belt ranking. For example, the black belts will be in the front of the class, followed by the red belts, the blue belts, the yellow belts, and finally the white belts. When several members of the school possess the same belt ranking, their order is determined by who has been a student of the school for the longest period of time.

## Bowing

Once the class has lined up, the instructor directs the students to face the flags. The flag of the home country and the flag of South Korea commonly hang on the walls of most dojangs. The students are then directed to bow to the flags.

**B**owing is an ancient Asian tradition and symbolizes respect. In the case of taekwondo, bowing to the flags symbolizes respect for one's own country and the country where taekwondo was born, South Korea. Bowing to the instructor and to other members of the class symbolizes respect for your fellow taekwondo practitioners.

A bow, in taekwondo, is accomplished by placing your hands, palms down, against your upper legs. You then slightly bend forward at waist level.

Once the bowing to the flags has been completed, the students are instructed to turn and face the instructor. They bow to the instructor, as he bows to them. The class may now get under way.

## *Kihap*

One commonly hears taekwondo practitioners performing a martial arts yell as they perform a technique. This yell is known in Korean as a *kihap*. The kihap is actually a conscious method for taekwondo practitioners to expel ki, internal energy, from their bodies as they perform a technique. This is understood to give the technique more power and cause practitioners to remain more focused. You perform the kihap by releasing your breath, in the form of a yell, from your central abdomenal region as you perform each technique.

All taekwondo students are instructed to perform a kihap in association with each technique they perform. Therefore, it is a good idea for the budding taekwondo practitioner to get into the habit of performing the kihap from the very beginning of training.

A *kihap* is the martial arts yell.

## Warmup

A taekwondo class begins with various forms of warmup exercises. The first traditional method of warming up is the horse stance middle punch (see Chapter 9). This exercise has the students enter into a horse stance and punch toward a central point.

Once this exercise is completed, the students are then directed to do push-ups on their knuckles. Commonly, the student is told to do ten push-ups.

Back on their feet, the class is then led through a series of leg-stretching exercises. As one of the elemental components of taekwondo is kicking, stretching is an essential part of the warmup. Stretching diminishes the chances that students will tear muscles while training.

## Blocking Practice

Blocking practice is usually the next level of training for the taekwondo class. Not only does blocking practice help to refine the students' skills, but it helps in the ongoing process of warming up.

What commonly occurs in blocking practice is that the instructor will direct the students to perform one of the taekwondo blocks: a low block, a high block, and so on. As each block is shouted out, the students will move forward and kihap while performing the individual block. When the lead member of the class reaches the wall, they will be instructed to pivot and turn around. The practice session will then continue, going the other way.

In some cases, where there is not adequate space for the students to move forward in lines, they will simply perform each block where they stand. When they are instructed to perform the next blocking technique, they will simply switch legs in a low jumping pattern, so that their rear leg takes the forward position.

The reason taekwondo students do push-ups on their knuckles is that this toughens the knuckles for punching.

## Punching Practice

Punching practice is usually the next level of training the class is guided through. To begin this segment of the class, the instructor will call out a command. For example, "Front stance, straight punch." With this, the students will kihap and follow through with the technique. The instructor will call out, "One, two, three, four," and the students will move forward, performing the technique, until they are instructed to perform another punching technique, or to stop.

## Incorporating Punching with Blocking

It is common in a taekwondo class to mix blocks and punches in the beginning training session. For example, an instructor may call out, "Low block, straight punch." With this, the class will move forward, performing a low block, then step forward while performing a straight punch.

From this, the students begin to learn how various combinations work together. Thereby, they begin to understand that no taekwondo technique is whole and complete unto itself.

# Kicking Practice

At the heart of taekwondo is its extensive kicking arsenal. For this reason, a large portion of every class is devoted to developing the legs.

The kicking segment of a taekwondo class commonly begins with the instructor leading the students through the stretch kick. To perform this kick, practitioners must powerfully lift one leg straight up, in order to gain a forced stretch.

Once this segment concludes, the class will be led through the basic kicks: front kick, side kick, and roundhouse kick. Although advancing students may question why they must continue to train with kicks they have already learned, continued training reinforces one's foundation in the art. In fact, advanced practitioners of taekwondo understand the need to go back and perform the basic kicks every day, to continually refine their advanced technique.

## Kicking Drills

Once the various single-kick techniques have been performed, the instructor will lead the class through multiple-kick techniques. He may call out, "Side kick, right leg, roundhouse kick, left leg." With this, the class will move forward and perform this combination technique.

## Punching and Kicking Drills

Punching may be added to these combinations, as well. The instructor may say, "Axe kick, right leg, back kick, left leg, straight punch, right arm." From doing this, the students will learn to integrate punches with their kicking techniques. Again, this trains the new student in effective taekwondo offensive combinations.

# Forms—*Poomse*

The Korean word *poomse* means "forms," the predetermined set of defensive and offensive movements.

Poomse is an essential element of taekwondo. It teaches the students how the various blocks, punches, and kicks are used in association with one another.

At the white-belt level, there are three forms that new students learn to introduce them to the basic blocks, punches, and kicks of taekwondo. As you advance through the ranks, each belt level has one additional form that is to be learned and mastered.

The word *poomse* is the Korean term used to describe the forms practiced in taekwondo.

Within each of these forms, the student is introduced to a new set of blocking, counterstriking, and striking combinations. This form training is designed to train the practitioner in the defensive and offensive applications of taekwondo.

During the poomse segment of the class, one of two scenarios occurs. In the first, the entire class is directed to perform the prescribed poomse. This begins with the class performing the most basic forms. As the more advanced poomse are called out, the lower belts sit down to the side of the training area as the higher belts perform their appropriate poomse.

In the second scenario, individual students are called up and asked to perform the poomse they are currently working on. This allows them to receive personal instruction on how their form performance may be improved.

## Self-Defense Training

As self-defense is the root of all martial arts training, once the forms segment of the class has been completed, many instructors will lead their students through a session of formalized self-defense techniques. In these self-defense applications, normally one student is on the offensive, and another on the defensive. The offensive student grabs the training partner in a specific manner—a choke hold, arm grab, or the like. The defensive student is then taught to respond to the attack in a very specific manner, ultimately disengaging the hold and striking the opponent in a debilitating manner.

## One-Step Sparring

For one-step sparring, the class breaks up into pairs. The students face off. The offensive student performs a front stance, low block, followed by a front stance, middle punch, with a kihap. The defending student then follows up with the same process. Once the defending student has signaled his or her readiness, the attacking student unleashes a single punch or kick. The defensive student then defends against that attack in a predetermined manner.

One-step sparring is made up of predetermined offensive and defensive applications. For example, the offensive student will perform "Straight punch, number 1." The defensive student will then counter that attack with a specific block and counterstriking measure. The students will then switch, and the other student will defend against the attack. The pair of students will then move on to "Straight punch, number 2." This process will continue until they have worked through all of the one-step sparring techniques appropriate to their belt level.

> One-step sparring teaches the taekwondo practitioner how to defend against the onslaught of a punching or kicking attack in the most efficient manner possible. The student is then capable of taking this knowledge to the streets if the need ever arises.

## Three-Step Sparring

For three-step sparring, pairs of students face off. In this drill, once the defending student has signaled his or her readiness with a down block, middle punch, and kihap, the attacking student unleashes three consecutive offensive techniques. These may include three kicks, three punches, or a combination of kicks and punches.

Three-step sparring allows students to develop an understanding of combination techniques. It also teaches them, through actual experience, which offensive technique most easily follows the previous applications.

## Sparring

Sparring in a taekwondo class takes place under the strict guidance of the instructor. Because sparring allows the student to actually experience what works in combative situations, it is an essential element of taekwondo training.

Sparring, in a taekwondo class, is generally limited to no-contact or semi-contact sparring. In no-contact sparring, the student directs an offensive technique toward a specific location on his or her training partner's body, and unleashes the technique, but does not actually make forceful contact with the punch or kick.

Semicontact sparring is generally only allowed once students have advanced through the ranks to blue-belt level and possess substantially more control over their techniques than novice students. In this style of sparring, the student directs an attack toward a specific location on the opponent's body, and strikes it lightly. From this, advancing taekwondo students not only learn to maintain control over their offensive techniques, but also develop the ability to target a strike on an opponent exactly.

Full-contact sparring is virtually never taught in the mixed-level taekwondo classroom. Full-contact training is relegated to a specific class, usually at black-belt level, where practitioners are trained in strictly competitive taekwondo skills.

## Meditation

Meditation is the single most important practice taekwondo stylists can undertake to focus their attention and to heighten their concentration.

Sitting or kneeling meditation is generally performed at the end of a taekwondo class. As the student's adrenaline is usually highly aroused by this point, the best style of meditation to perform is to simply close your eyes and consciously take in several very deep breaths. This will instantly calm you down, refocusing your energy and preparing you for other life activities.

The word *munyum* is the Korean term used to describe meditation.

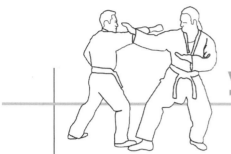

# chapter 7
# your first class

**Y**OUR FIRST CLASS in taekwondo is an exciting, adrenaline-filled experience. You will be entering into a new world—a world that you have no doubt seen in countless moments on television and in the movies, but have not personally experienced.

## Training Begins

Prior to beginning your first class, you will be instructed in the basic protocols of taekwondo. Commonly, an assistant instructor will be assigned to you to detail these essential elements of taekwondo.

You will be instructed in the appropriate techniques of respect, which are adhered to in all schools of taekwondo. You will be taught that you must immediately bow upon entering the martial art studio. This bowing symbolizes that you are formally demonstrating respect for your school.

You will be taught that upon entering the school you must also immediately remove your shoes. The reason shoes are removed in a school of taekwondo is to both demonstrate respect for the school and to symbolize that you are entering a training hall.

Once your shoes have been removed and you have entered the school, you will then be taught that you must bow to your instructor or instructors before you progress toward the dressing room where you will change into your uniform. Bowing to your instructor is also an essential sign of respect.

The assistant instructor will then teach you how to wear the taekwondo uniform and how to tie your belt properly. You will then be ready to immerse yourself in the exciting training of taekwondo.

Before your first class begins the assistant instructor will teach you some of the basic movements of taekwondo. You will be taught how to safely perform some of the preliminary stretching techniques and some of the basic blocks, kicks, and punches of taekwondo.

Once these preliminary elements have been detailed, your first class will begin. You will be taught to line up in the appropriate placement and you will be led through the basic bowing and warmup exercises.

In many schools of taekwondo, an assistant instructor will stand by you throughout your first class. This is done in order to aid in your indoctrination into the basic elements of taekwondo.

At the point the warmup segment of the class has culminated, an assistant instructor will again take you to the side where you will be privately trained in the basic blocking, kicking, and punching techniques of taekwondo. As your first class progresses, you may be teamed up with another new student in order that you will get the feel of actually performing some of the techniques of taekwondo against another body. Your first class will culminate with your peers and yourself reforming into prescribed lines, where the final bow of the class takes place.

The other common experience after the first class in taekwondo is to wake up the next day very, very sore. Taekwondo is a cardioaerobic-based system of self-defense that will cause you to exercise in a method you have not previously experienced. It will also cause you to use muscles that previously were dormant. As a result, when you cultivate these undeveloped muscles, there will definitely be a sense of soreness. Again, this is nothing to be worried about, and it will pass after a few days of training.

In earlier periods of time, the martial art training hall was considered to be a holy sanctuary.

It is essential to understand at the outset of your training that there are two distinct levels of taekwondo instruction. The first is that of self-defense. Taekwondo is a highly refined system of self-defense that teaches its practitioners to rapidly and effectively defend themselves if they are ever physically attacked. The second level of taekwondo training involves tournament competition. Many of the taekwondo techniques taught as a means of self-defense cannot be used in tournament competition, as they are too physically debilitating to the opponent and would violate tournament rules and policies.

From the beginning stages forward, a taekwondo practitioner must learn to differentiate between these two areas of the art—using each in its appropriate capacity.

Do not be surprised, when you return home from your first class, if you realize that you have forgotten everything that you were taught. Don't worry, this is a very common experience. After a few more classes, the techniques will become engraved in your mind.

# chapter 8
# safety

**Y**OUR SAFETY IS the most important element when you begin your training in taekwondo. If you are unnecessarily injured, your training will be sidelined and you will not be able to continue your exploration of this exciting system of self-defense.

As taekwondo is a very physical sport, an untold number of injuries can happen while training. Although there is no way to ensure that you will not be injured, there are a couple of simple things that you can do to protect yourself.

## Stretching

At the beginning of every taekwondo class, the students are led through stretching exercises. Often, new students who arrive at class early will immediately begin to throw high kicks, instead of stretching. This is one of the quickest ways to tear your muscles. A torn muscle can keep you on the sidelines for days or even weeks, so you must always stretch before you perform even the most basic technique.

Stretching is the single most important thing you can do in order to keep your body safe and free from muscle tearing injury.

## Train at Your Own Level

The next safety policy you must follow is to train at your own level. Do not attempt black-belt techniques when you have just earned your yellow belt. Do not attempt to perform advanced flying kicks until you have mastered the basic kicking techniques. Do not throw your front kick as high in the air as possible, causing yourself to lose your balance and end up on the ground—possibly breaking your wrist as you attempt to catch your fall.

Of course, you want to excel in the art, and grow as a taekwondo practitioner—but do so in a controlled manner. This will keep you healthy, so that you can master the basic techniques and then move on to the more advanced exercises, while remaining free from injury.

## Protective Gear and Safety

It is essential to remember that injuring your body serves no purpose. If you want to wear protective gear, do so. It may keep you free from injury.

There is protective gear that is associated with taekwondo and can help you remain free from injury: chest protectors, groin cups, shin guards, forearm guards, and foot pads, just to name a few. However, you will not normally witness most of these protective items being worn in a taekwondo class because they are too restrictive for everyday training.

## Broken Bones and Torn Ligaments

It is very easy to break your bones or tear your ligaments while training in taekwondo. This can occur from any number of factors. You can kick one of your opponent's protruding joints, while sparring, and break your foot. You can land incorrectly from a jumping kick and break your ankle or rip the ligaments of your knee. You can incorrectly block the oncoming kick of a training partner and break your arm, wrist, hand, or finger. During sparring, your fellow student may kick you in a joint, causing it to break or tear.

At the outset, you must understand that all of this bone breaking and ligament tearing can occur while you are training in taekwondo. No doubt, your instructor will do everything he can do to prevent you from being injured, but, there is virtually no one who has travelled down the road of taekwondo without breaking a bone during training or being injured in some way.

There is no foolproof method to keep yourself free from injury while training in taekwondo, but you can limit your chances of injury considerably by remaining as mindful of your individual movements as possible. Therefore, perform every defensive or offensive action with as much awareness as possible. From this style of training, not only will you become a more proficient taekwondo practitioner, but you may also avoid unnecessary injury.

Ultimately, it is you who must make the choices that will keep you safe in this very physical style of self-defense. By remaining prudent and conscious during all of your actions in the taekwondo class, hopefully you will keep your injuries to a minimum and continue to enjoy training in the art.

# part 3
# learning the basics

**W**HEN ONE THINKS of taekwondo, its vast arsenal of kicking techniques is commonly the first thought that comes to mind. Although its advanced kicks have come to define this art, taekwondo is much more than simply a style of martial arts that emphasizes the feet. Taekwondo is an advanced system of self-defense that leads its practitioners to levels of physical mastery never experienced by the average individual. It does this by teaching them to train their bodies in a unique and ever-expanding manner that allows them to transcend normal forms of physical movement and achieve new realms of physical perfection.

<br />

# chapter 9
# stances

**A**T THE HEART of any taekwondo technique is the stance, or *sogi*. The stance is the most essential element to the execution of any technique, because if you do not launch your techniques from a proper stance, you can easily lose your balance and fall. Additionally, if you are not locked into a strong stance while unleashing an offensive technique, you may quickly be overpowered by your opponent. Thus, a proper stance is the essential element to all of your taekwondo training.

## Ready Stance

The first stance taught in taekwondo is the ready stance, *chunbe sogi*. This is a very simple stance that is used as a formality before actual training begins.

The ready stance is performed by standing with your feet naturally separated at one shoulders' width, and your toes pointing forward. Your hands are made into fists and held at waist level, approximately six inches in front of your body. Your back is straight, and your focus is directly in front of you.

**A** taekwondo instructor will ready the class for practice by calling out the command, "Chunbe!" The class will then enter into the ready stance, as the instructor tells the students what technique they are about to perform.

## The Horse Stance

The horse stance, *ju chum sogi*, is the foundational stance for taekwondo. Many of the basic techniques are performed while in this stance.

To enter into a horse stance, separate your legs to approximately two shoulders'

Figure 9-1: Horse stance, middle punch

width. Your toes should point forward. Lower yourself into this stance by bending your knees.

## Horse Stance, Middle Punch

Virtually every taekwondo class begins with the horse stance, middle punch—*ju chum sogi ap chigi*—warmup (see Figure 9-1). This is one of taekwondo's primary techniques.

To perform this technique, enter into the horse stance. Make your hands into fists. Place one of your fists at belt level on your side. The palm of this hand should be facing upward. Place your other fist directly in front of you, at solar plexus level. The palm of this hand should be facing the floor.

The command is called out: "One." At this, extend the fist that is at your waist, while you retract the fist that was extended. Allow your fists to pivot in midair, so that when the fist you are retracting reaches your waist it is facing upward, and the fist that you are extending is facing downward. "Two." Again, perform this process, extending your waist-level fist as your forward fist is recoiled.

The purpose of this horse stance exercise is for novice students to begin to gain control over the elements of their bodies. First, they begin to learn focus as they are focusing their punch on a very precise target—the solar plexus level of the body. Second, they are learning coordination—as one fist retracts in an upward position, the other fist is extended in a downward position.

## Horse Stance Meditation

As one advances in taekwondo, the horse stance becomes a tool not only for focus and coordination training but for bodily development and meditation, as well. Horse stance meditation technique, *ju chum sogi munyum*, is commonly taught to the advancing student of taekwondo.

To perform this technique, enter into a deep horse stance. Make both of your hands into fists, and place them at belt level, palms facing upward. You will remain in this stance for a prescribed amount of time—usually fifteen minutes, in the beginning. As you advance, this allotment of time may go up to one hour.

The reason a taekwondo practitioner performs the horse stance meditation is that, first of all, this is a very important method of training the mind of the practitioner to focus. It requires discipline to remain in this stance for more than a few minutes. As the disciplined taekwondo practitioner is commonly the one who excels, this simple exercise goes a long way in refining the mind and the body of the student for success in the art.

Second, this stance is a very efficient method of gaining leg strength. As much of taekwondo's curriculum involves legwork, this is an easy method to tone the muscles of the legs and add muscle mass.

## The Front Stance

The front stance, *ap sogi*, is an essential element to all of taekwondo offensive and defensive methodology. Although it is a rudimentary stance, it is used throughout the taekwondo curriculum.

To perform a front stance, move one leg forward as if you were taking a long step. Allow your forward knee to bend, as you straighten your rear leg. The toes of your forward foot should be pointing straight ahead. Your rear foot should be allowed to angle slightly outward. The spacing of your legs should be approximately one shoulders' width.

The taekwondo front stance is used in association with such defensive techniques as the down block, side block, and up block. It is also used for stability when such offensive techniques as the straight punch or reverse punch are unleashed.

## The Back Stance

The back stance, *dui gubi sogi*, is performed by separating your feet at a walking distance. You then shift approximately 75 percent of your weight to your rear leg. Your rear foot turns outward, as your forward foot points straight ahead. This positioning should cause your two feet to make the shape of the letter "L."

The taekwondo back stance is used in association with such blocks as the knife-hand middle block. It is also an effective tool in sparring, to protect yourself from having your legs swept from underneath you. With 75 percent of your weight on your rear leg, if you do experience a sweep kick to your forward leg, you will be able to maintain your balance.

Figure 9-2: Fighting stance

# The Fighting Stance

The fighting stance, *gyoo rugi sogi* (see Figure 9-2), has you standing with legs naturally apart, maintaining a generalized balance. Your elbows are bent at a forty-five-degree angle and are suspended at midtorso level— a few inches away from the body. Your hands are formed into fists. One arm, referred to as the lead arm, is generally higher and out in front of your other arm. Your rear arm maintains a rear protective positioning.

The fighting stance is used in training when the taekwondo practitioner is practicing the various punches and kicks. It is also used in sparring, to maintain readiness to protect against any oncoming attack or to unleash an offensive assault.

## The Combative Side-Fighting Stance

Taekwondo is a scientific system of self-defense. As such, each component of its offensive and defensive arsenal is precisely studied in order to refine each element to the degree where it is most effective in all forms of combat. This is also the case with the fighting stance.

Virtually all systems of self-defense dictate that when you enter into a fighting stance, you do so by facing your opponent with your lead side forward, and your body at a forty-five-degree angle. This common formula is not the case, however, with taekwondo's combative side-fighting stance, *yup gyoo rugi sogi* (see Figure 9-3).

When combat is imminent, whether in the gym or on the street, the taekwondo practitioner turns his or her body to the degree that only the side is exposed. This leaves much less target area for the opponent to strike. In addition, ease in retreating from an attack or rapidly moving forward is amplified because the body is in a position where it can quickly slide back or slide in, as necessary.

Figure 9-3: Combative side-fighting stance                Figure 9-4: Low fighting stance

## Low Fighting Stance

To perform the low fighting stance, *natchoom gyoo rugi sogi,* you begin by entering into the combative side-fighting stance. You then lower yourself down, by bending your knees approximately 30 percent more than in the normal fighting stance.

The low fighting stance is a combative technique. It is ideally used when you are observing your opponent's movements, and you wish to rapidly strike out at him with an offensive flurry.

The word *sogi* is the Korean term used to describe stances. The main stances are *chunbe sogi,* which means "ready stance"; *ju chum sogi,* which means "horse stance"; *ap sogi,* which means "front stance"; *dui gubi sogi,* which means "back stance"; and *gyoo rugi sogi,* which means "fighting stance."

**T**HE OFFENSIVE METHODOLOGY of taekwondo possesses an elaborate array of kicking and punching techniques. Offense cannot ensure your victory in a competition, however, so precise blocking techniques are added to the martial arts arsenal of each taekwondo student.

Blocking a punch or a kick is more than simply stopping the assault of an opponent. Though blocking will not defeat an attacker, it is designed to provide you with a method of redirecting the attack of an opponent, thereby giving you the opportunity to make a successful counterattack.

In the dojang, the taekwondo student is taught to perform blocks in a traditional and formalized manner. That is, the quality of a student's block is judged by proper form in both stance and blocking technique. It is essential to understand, however, that in competition the structured form of a block is relaxed. The taekwondo practitioner takes the essence of the block, loosens it up to fit the situation, and unleashes it in the most effective manner possible.

## The Low Block

The taekwondo low block, *arae makki* (see Figure 10-1), is performed by initially entering into a front stance. Simultaneously, make your hands into fists. Extend your forward arm downward, across the front of your body. Your blocking arm

Figure 10-1: The low block

comes to rest directly above your forward leg. Your nonblocking hand comes to rest, in an upward-facing fist, at your belt level.

This style of block will defeat any attack that has been directed toward the lower region of your body. It ideally counters such attacks as the front kick.

Figure 10-2: High block

## High Block

The taekwondo high block, *ohgul makki* (see Figure 10-2), is performed as you enter into a front stance. You make your hands into fists, as you simultaneously bring your lead arm across the front of your body—from waist-level up.

The high block culminates with your blocking arm reaching its final position above your head, relatively parallel to the ground. Your nonblocking hand comes to rest, with an upward-facing fist, at your belt level.

This high block is designed to block any attack directed at the top of your head. It ideally stops overhead club assaults.

The word *makki* is the Korean term used to describe the blocks of taekwondo. The main blocks are *arae makki*, which means "low block"; *ohgul makki*, which means "high block"; *anpalmok olgul bakkat makki*, which means "middle block"; *soonal momtong makki*, which means "knife-hand middle block"; *soonal ale makki*, which means "knife-hand low block"; *otgorea area makki*, which means "low X block"; and *aolgul otgorea makki*, which means "high X block."

Figure 10-3: Middle block

Figure 10-4: Knife-hand middle block

# Middle Block

The middle block, *anpalmok olgul bakkat makki* (see Figure 10-3), is performed as you enter into a front stance. Make your hands into fists. Bend your blocking arm at the elbow and swing it in from the outside of your body. Your nonblocking hand comes to rest, in an upward-facing fist, at belt level.

This block is designed to intercept oncoming punches. It will easily deflect an oncoming straight punch.

# Knife-Hand Middle Block

The knife-hand middle block, *soonal momtong makki* (see Figure 10-4), is performed by making both of your hands into knife hands. As you do so, enter into a back stance. Then bring your knife hands in across your central body, in a sweeping fashion. This block culminates with the lead hand blocking a punching attack that was unleashed toward your central body or your head, and your rear hand remaining above your solar plexus.

# Knife-Hand Low Block

This same blocking technique is used in a low pattern, *soonal ale makki*, to defend against the onslaught of a kicking attack.

Figure 10-5: Low X block

# X Block (Low)

The low X block, *otgoreo arae makki* (see Figure 10-5), is a technique designed to intercept low attacks, such as that of an oncoming front kick. To achieve this, you rapidly cross your arms, at wrist level, as you step forward into a front stance. This will then intercept the force of the kick.

# X Block (High)

Figure 10-6: High X block

The high X block, *olgul otgoreo makki* (see Figure 10-6), is actualized in a pattern similar to that of the low X block. This technique is very effective in foiling the onslaught of an axe kick or the downward strike of a club.

To execute the high X block, rapidly move into a front stance, as your crossed, fisted hands move upward across the front of your body. This technique culminates with a crossed-arm interception of your attacker's leg or arm.

# hand and arm
# strikes

**A**s it is natural for you to begin to defend yourself with your hands and your fists, it is imperative that you learn how to use them most effectively.

Taekwondo is most noted for its advanced kicking arsenal, but it also possesses a large array of precise hand and arm strikes. In Korean, the term *chigi* is used to describe a taekwondo punching technique. As is the case with the taekwondo kick, each of these techniques is designed to be unleashed in the most economical and straight-to-the-target manner possible. In this way, an opponent is most efficiently defeated.

Figure 11-1: Straight punch

## The Straight Punch

The straight punch, *juchumso chigi* (see Figure 11-1), is a highly linear offensive technique. In a straight punch, your fist is launched from your shoulder and is directed straight toward its target, with your fist horizontal to the ground.

The straight punch is ideally delivered when the elbow of your punching arm remains slightly bent upon making impact with its target. This is accomplished by accurately judging the distance and hitting your objective before your arm reaches the point where it must stretch or extend unnaturally to reach the desired strike point. By allowing your elbow to remain slightly bent whenever you utilize a straight punch, you not only maintain maximum body balance but you also keep your elbow from possible hyperextension, as the momentum of the punch drives it forward.

Making contact with your target before you have fully extended your punching arm is the primary element that gives the straight punch its devastating power. If the distance the punch has to travel is kept as short as possible, you can continue forward with the force and power of the punch, extending it deeply into your target. If, on the other hand, you have to reach to make contact with your opponent, you will expend much of the power of your punch before it ever strikes its target.

## The Straight Punch versus the Roundhouse Punch

The reason the straight punch is the preferential punching technique for self-defense applications is that it is extremely fast and difficult to defend against. As such, it holds several advantages over the more common roundhouse punch. For example, in the roundhouse punch, the punching arm first swings outward and then in toward its target. For this reason, the roundhouse punch is not only much slower than the straight punch, but also much more obvious and easy to defend against.

Figure 11-2: Palm strike

## The Palm Strike

The palm strike, *batongson chigi* (see Figure 11-2), like the straight punch, is delivered in a linear fashion. For the palm strike, you bend your fingers at your second knuckle, which exposes the base of your palm. Bending your fingers in this fashion tightens the muscle that extends from your thumb across the base of your hand. This provides you with a powerful striking weapon.

Your palm is then brought back to your shoulder level. The technique is unleashed by snapping the strike toward your target with your shoulder muscles.

The palm strike is most effectively

used to target locations on your opponent's head, such as underneath the base of his nose, which can prove deadly, across the bridge of his nose, his temples, or the side of his jaw.

Figure 11-3: Knife hand

## The Knife Hand

To form the knife hand, *soonal* (see Figure 11-3), your fingers are extended and the muscles and tendons in your hand and wrist are tightened. The basic strike weapon of the knife hand is the base of your hand, which extends from the end of your wrist to the point where your little finger begins.

The knife-hand strike is propelled by the extension of your arm and then the snapping out of your elbow. The momentum developed by the snapping out of your elbow should never be allowed to entirely control your knife-hand assault. The elbow should remain slightly bent when the knife-hand technique is delivered, so that you maintain control over your movement.

The mistake many individuals make, when first attempting to use the knife hand as a weapon, is to relax the tension in their hand either just before or during the knife-hand strike. This should never be done; by making this mistake, you can easily break the bones of your hand.

Unlike the fist, the knife hand cannot be used to strike virtually anywhere on an opponent, with the hope of having a cumulative effect. Instead, the knife hand is ideally suited to strike very specific locations on an opponent's body: the front of his neck, across his nose, to his temples, and the side of his ribs.

## Reverse Knife Hand

The reverse knife hand, *soonal deung* (see Figure 11-4), is a very specific striking weapon. Like the traditional knife hand, the reverse knife hand must be aimed at precise locations on your opponent's body.

Figure 11-4: Reverse knife hand

To form the reverse knife hand, make your hand into a knife hand, and then press your thumb deeply into the palm of your hand. The striking portion of this weapon is along the inside of your hand.

The reverse knife hand is ideally targeted at the nose, throat, or neck, or when used in an upward striking motion, the groin of your opponent.

# The Elbow Strike

The elbow strike, *pal kup*, is a close-contact fighting weapon. It has two applications: the forward elbow strike and the rear elbow strike.

## The Forward Elbow Strike

For the forward elbow strike, you bend your elbow, exposing the protruding elbow bone at the base of your forearm. This bone is your striking tool. The elbow strike is ideally aimed at vital strike points on your opponent's head.

To perform the forward elbow strike, bring your elbow up to shoulder level and strike your target by pivoting your body at waist level and, if possible, stepping in with your lead foot.

The forward elbow strike is an ideal tool for close-contact fighting if you find that your opponent has taken a powerful forward hold on your body, and his temple or face is exposed.

## The Rear Elbow Strike

The rear elbow strike is an ideal weapon to use if an attacker has grabbed hold of your body from behind. If you have been grabbed from behind, use the rear elbow strike by pivoting backward, unleashing your bent elbow from shoulder level, and striking virtually any part of your attacker's body.

If you have not yet been grabbed from behind, but your attacker is close, you can add the additional momentum-driven force of your body to the strike by pivoting at your waist level as your rear elbow strike is unleashed.

Figure 11-5: Forward elbow strike

Figure 11-6: Rear elbow strike

The main taekwondo hand and arm strikes are *juchumso chigi*, which means "straight punch"; *batongson chigi*, which means "palm strike"; *soonal*, which means "knife hand"; *soonal deung*, which means "reverse knife hand"; and *pal kup*, which means "forward elbow strike."

# kicking

F OR A TAEKWONDO kicking technique to be effective as a combative tool, it must be fast, difficult to block, and able to proceed to its target in the most efficient manner possible. To this end, taekwondo kicking techniques are designed to meet these requirements—each with its own unique purpose and application.

## Kicking Preliminaries

You use both of your legs whenever you perform a kicking technique: Your base leg is the leg that balances you and anchors your body to the ground. Your striking leg is the one that actually delivers the kick.

T he word *chagi* is the Korean term used to describe the taekwondo kick.
The main kicks are *ap chagi*, which means "front kick"; *yup chagi*, which means "side kick"; *dollo chagi*, which means "roundhouse kick"; *nerya chagi*, which means "axe kick"; *gullgi chagi*, which means "hook kick"; and *dwei chagi*, which means "back kick."

### The Base Leg

Whenever you begin a kicking technique, you should allow the heel of the foot of your base leg to be raised slightly upward, approximately half an inch off the ground. This is accomplished by allowing your toes to bend slightly, as you come up on the ball of your foot. Kicking techniques are most efficiently performed from the ball of the foot, because this lets your body maintain maximum mobility while the actual technique is in motion. By performing your kicks in this fashion, you also allow your foot to pivot into appropriate position while your kick proceed toward its target—keeping you in balance throughout the execution of the technique.

The knee of your base leg should be slightly bent whenever you perform a kicking technique. This adds to the overall balance of your body; you will be able to adjust your position easily, by adding more or less bend to your knee, to compensate for the height and velocity of your kick.

The slightly bent knee of the base leg also helps you recover quickly from your kicking technique. If the knee of your base leg remained locked into a straight-up position as you performed any kicking technique, the tendons, the cartilage, or the knee itself could easily be damaged.

> If you were to lock your entire foot firmly on the ground, as some martial arts systems teach, your ankle would become inflexible. This could result in injury to your ankle and the bones of your foot, due to the fact that other portions of your body were rapidly shifting to compensate for the muscle-driven momentum and power of your kicking technique.

## The Striking Leg

In taekwondo, the striking leg is never allowed to fully extend when a kicking technique is performed. The knee of the striking leg should remain slightly bent. This is accomplished by maintaining muscle control over the lower part of your leg, and not allowing the momentum of the kick to force your leg to extend unnecessarily.

Because the knee joint is one of the most sensitive joints of the human body, be sure to keep both knees slightly bent, to prevent them from hyperextending or bending backward unnaturally.

## The Rear Leg
## or the Forward (Lead) Leg

Many traditional martial arts systems launch their kicking techniques solely from the rear leg. It is believed that performing a kick in this fashion will substantially increase the momentum and power of the kick. Although there is truth to this opinion, launching kicking techniques only from the rear leg slows the kicks down considerably. For the sake of increased speed and additional overall effectiveness, a taekwondo kick can be launched from either the rear or the forward leg—which to use is determined only by which will prove more effective. Thus, the taekwondo practitioner is better able to tailor each kick to match each self-defense situation.

# The Front Kick

The front kick, *ap chagi*, is the first kick that all taekwondo students are trained to perform. Although it is the most elementary offensive kicking technique, it becomes one of the most devastatingly effective offensive or defensive techniques in your kicking arsenal, when performed correctly.

## Launching the Basic Front Kick

The basic front kick is performed by entering into a traditional fighting stance, with your fists clenched in front of you. You then launch your rear leg forward by rapidly raising the knee of your striking leg up to approximately your hip level (Figure 12-1a). The lower section of your striking leg is then immediately snapped outward in the direction of the kicking target (Figure 12-1b). The front kick's power is developed by a combination of upper-leg muscle strength and lower-leg snapping momentum.

Figure 12-1a: Launching the basic front kick, Part 1    Figure 12-1b: Launching the basic front kick, Part 2

The impact of the front kick can be made with either the instep of your foot or the ball of your foot. The latter is accomplished by pulling back your toes, exposing the ball of your foot.

Performing the front kick with the ball of the foot is more advanced and takes additional practice. Through continued practice, however, the ability to instantly pull back your toes will become quite natural.

It is very important to pull back your toes when kicking in this fashion, even if you are wearing shoes. If your toes are allowed to remain in their naturally extended position, they can easily be broken when target impact is made.

## Retracting the Front Kick

Japanese martial arts systems generally teach their students to retract the front kick with the same snapping speed and velocity with which it is delivered. Taekwondo, on the other hand, does not perform the front kick in this fashion. Instead, a front kick is powerfully extended toward its target. Once impact has been made, the striking leg is allowed to remain in position for a millisecond, in order to deliver the full energy of the kick to the target.

If a front kick is retracted with the same speed with which it is delivered, it will lose much of its impact energy, because of the rapid snapping back of the leg. Therefore, to deliver the full power of any front kick, snap your leg into its target with full force. Then, do not allow its forward momentum to snap the lower section of your striking leg back. Instead, take conscious control over the muscles of your lower leg, and allow the kick to retract in a controlled fashion.

> Unlike karate, taekwondo stresses the importance of momentarily keeping your striking leg in position after reaching your target in order to deliver the full impact of the kick.

When learning proper front-kick delivery, the taekwondo student is taught to consciously retract the lower portion of the striking leg, only a few inches, after performing a front kick. This is accomplished by allowing the upper leg to remain semiextended at the hip joint once the kick has been unleashed. From this position, the student consciously allows the kicking foot to drop to the ground, forming a forward stance. In this way, the student learns to properly deliver the front kick and utilize its power.

### Mistakes with the Front Kick

Most taekwondo students learn how to perform the basic front kick soon after they begin their training. Instead of focusing on the best way to use this simple, yet very effective, kick, however, most students concentrate on how high they can deliver their front kick. This is the first mistake in proper front-kick development, made by many new taekwondo students.

With opening class warmups, the novice taekwondo students will generally attempt to front kick as high into the air as possible. Beginners often learn the hard way that they have not yet developed the proper balance to deliver a high front kick. What generally happens is that these students awkwardly fall down backward. This lack of balance is largely due to the fact that they have remained flatfooted while performing this kicking technique.

When you perform the basic front kick correctly, the momentum that launches the kick forward should also move your entire body forward, so you rise slightly up onto the ball of the foot of your base leg. As you raise your heel slightly off the ground, allow your nonkicking knee to bend slightly. In this way, your body is allowed to naturally balance itself, preventing you from falling.

Once you have learned to perform the front kick correctly, you can concentrate on the height of your kick. Remember, however, that high kicking does little to prepare you for a confrontational situation. You will rarely need to kick above your head while fighting. For this reason, focusing your technique on an imaginary target at the level of your solar plexus is a far more effective method of front-kick training than simply seeing how high the momentum of your front kick will take your leg.

## Focusing the Front Kick

The basic front kick is an ideal close-contact fighting weapon. It is perfect to unleash against an opponent who has faced off with you and is in very close proximity to your body.

As is commonly understood, a front kick to the groin of any individual is universally debilitating. Other close-contact front-kick targets are the solar plexus, the stomach, or the underside of your adversary's jaw.

## Redesigning the Basic Front Kick

There is one primary flaw to the basic front kick, and that is its range. If your opponent moves slightly backward, out of the upward-driven path of attack, the basic front kick misses. This problem is predominantly caused by the novice practitioner's tendency, as discussed, to allow the front kick's momentum to drive the kick upward—as opposed to inward, toward a target.

To develop the ability to make the front kick truly effective, you must refocus it at a target that will not be easily missed. Begin in a fighting stance. Prepare to launch a basic front kick from your rear leg. Instead of focusing the power of this kick upward, focus it deeply in toward the solar-plexus level of an imaginary opponent in front of you. Now, launch your front kick toward your imaginary target.

Simply by extending your front kick in this fashion, you will easily cover the distance between yourself and an opponent, to make contact. With this simple refocusing technique, you will make the basic front kick much more effective.

Figure 12-2: Leaning-back front kick

## The Leaning-Back Front Kick

The leaning-back front kick is the first modification of the basic front kick that is taught to the taekwondo student. This kick is an ideal weapon to use during sparring matches, and sparring is a central focus of taekwondo training.

To perform the leaning-back front kick, simply unleash a front kick in the traditional manner, focusing in toward your opponent. As you do so, simultaneously lean your body back at waist level.

What this does is extend the distance between your opponent's body and your own. This allows him less chance to strike you in your upper body or face—the two areas where contact is permitted in taekwondo sparring matches. As a result, you may well gain a point, without providing your opponent with the same opportunity.

## The Momentum-Driven Front Kick

You now understand the factors that help you to launch a successful basic front kick. By slightly altering this kick, you can take it to the next level—making it a truly effective offensive and defensive weapon.

To achieve this, you must first understand that the front kick is not limited to the distance your striking leg can extend from its starting position. There is no reason in any confrontational situation for you to remain firmly planted and locked into any location. This is the first lesson to learn in extending the range of your front kick.

Suppose you have faced off with an opponent who is several feet in front of you. You are both in fighting stances, with your fists raised. The common tactic is to cautiously move in toward your opponent and then begin the combat. Although this type of encounter is common, it is no doubt the quickest way to lose a fight.

Instead of graciously facing off and moving slowly in toward your opponent, why not take advantage of his stationary position? One of the most effective ways of achieving this is with the momentum-driven front kick.

The front kick, by its very nature, is a very direct, linear kick. It has the ability to penetrate your opponent's defenses quickly and easily. It can shoot in, under your opponent's clenched fists, and deliver a powerful blow to his midsection before he even knows what hit him. This can set the stage for your victory in the confrontation.

Extend the range of your front kick by allowing the momentum of its launch to drive you forward.

Although the elementary front kick has little distance or range capabilities, this same kicking technique can be slightly altered to give you substantial distance for attacking your opponent. To achieve this, begin by entering into a fighting stance. Ready yourself to perform a front kick. Now, instead of performing this front kick as a stationary technique, as you have done in the past, visualize a target several feet in front of yourself. As you snap your front kick outward, allow the momentum-driven power of this kick to pull your body forward. Do not attempt to control or compensate for this experience. Simply allow yourself to be pulled forward by the momentum your striking leg unleashes, sliding your base foot along the ground. Do not attempt to hinder this forward motion. Let it move you closer in toward your target. This type of front-kicking technique gives you not only additional range, but additional power as well, because the force of your body weight is moving in toward your target.

As you practice this momentum-driven front kick, you will come to realize that you can effortlessly travel several feet in toward your opponent without ever losing your balance. Then, the next time you and an opponent face off, you can immediately drive forward with a momentum-driven front kick, deliver it under his guard, and powerfully strike the first blow in the competition.

###  *Mistakes of the Momentum–Driven Front Kick*

The leading mistake people make when attempting the momentum-driven front kick is extending the snapping motion of their lower leg before they are in range of their target. This dissipates the power of their kick before it has the opportunity to impact its target. Additionally, by unleashing the momentum-driven front kick in this premature fashion, the taekwondo practitioner stands the chance of hyperextending his or her own knee in the process. Therefore, to make the momentum-driven front kick a viable offensive technique, you should never extend the lower portion of your striking leg until you are very close to your target and sure of making contact.

## The Defensive Front Kick

The front kick is a very rapid and penetrating weapon. When it is employed in defensive applications, not only do you halt any attack that is launched against you, but the defensive force of your kick more than likely prevents your attacker from launching any secondary attack, as well.

The best time to launch a defensive front kick is when your opponent is in the midst of launching his offensive attack.

The best opportunity to launch a defensive front kick is when your opponent is in the midst of his offensive action. He will be unable to rapidly redirect the motion of his offensive technique while it is in progress, nor will he be able to readily block your defensive kick. Thus, he will be in a vulnerable position to be counterattacked with the full power of your front kick.

### Front Kick versus a Charging Attacker

The defensive front kick is a very simple and effective weapon to use in many confrontational situations. Suppose an attacker is charging in at you. When he is in close range, simply deliver a basic front kick to his midsection. His advance is halted, he may be injured, and you can leave the site of the altercation or follow up with additional self-defense, as necessary.

### Front Kick versus a Spinning Heel Kick

To further understand the ease of using the defensive front kick, you can look at using it to defend against the spinning heel kick or the straight back kick. For either of these two kicks to be successfully delivered, your opponent must turn around. As he is in the process of making this turn, you have the opportunity to use the front kick as a defensive tool and halt his attack altogether. This is most readily accomplished by simply delivering a front kick to your adversary's buttocks, as he spins around. When you deliver this well-placed front kick, your opponent's kick is immediately stopped, and he will be thrown off balance. Commonly, he will be sent to the ground.

> **S**igns that a punching attack is about to begin are:
>
> ☞ the pulling back of the shoulder before a roundhouse punch, and
>
> ☞ the lowering of the elbow before a straight punch.

### Front Kick versus a Roundhouse Kick

Suppose an opponent launches a roundhouse kick at you. Due to the circular, momentum-driven nature of this kicking technique, it develops its power by first travelling away, and then in toward its target. As the front kick is completely linear, you can quickly deliver a defensive front kick to your opponent's midsection before his roundhouse kick can reach its target. Thus, not only have you delivered the first strike to your opponent, but you have interrupted his kick and no doubt sent him backward, possibly to the ground. From this point, additional counterstriking measures may be launched, if necessary.

## The Low Front Kick

To begin to understand the defensive front kick, you can view one of its most basic applications, that of the low front kick. The low front kick is a very effective first-line defensive tool.

The low front kick is executed in the same fashion as the basic front kick, but it is targeted at lower locations. An ideal location is your opponent's shin.

A front-kick shin strike, though obviously not as devastating as a groin strike, is nonetheless very effective in deterring an opponent from launching an initial offensive attack against you. Your opponent moves toward you. Immediately, you deliver a low front kick, targeted at his shin. From this impact, his attack is halted and you can either follow up with additional defensive countermeasures, as necessary, or leave the situation before the altercation continues any further.

### Low Front Kick versus a Kicking Attack

The low front kick technique is also an effective weapon for defensively intercepting the onslaught of an opponent's front kick. Suppose you have faced off with an adversary, and he begins to launch a front kick at you. Immediately, you deliver a low front kick to the shin region of his striking leg before it has the opportunity to travel toward you.

This halts his kicking attack, and your opponent is unprepared to rapidly launch a secondary assault at you, because his offensive technique has been intercepted. From your position, however, you are ready to strike at him with a well-prepared secondary counterstrike, such as a straight punch to the face.

The low front kick is a very easy kick to deliver to your opponent, because your front striking leg only needs to rise slightly from the ground. Therefore, this kick is extremely fast and highly energy-efficient. To be effective, however, the low front kick must be precisely targeted. This type of precision comes from target-kicking drills focused at low levels.

## The Advanced Defensive Front Kick

As you begin to refine the use of the defensive front kick, you will want to watch for certain physical gestures an opponent will make just prior to launching an attack. From these, you will know when it is time to unleash your defensive front kick. Ideally, you will learn to recognize these gestures when studying the elements that make up the various punching assaults.

The common signs that a punching attack is about to begin are (1) the pulling back of the shoulder before a roundhouse punch, and (2) the lowering of the elbow before launching a straight punch. These subtle motions are signs to watch for at the start of any physical confrontation. They will alert you as to what type of punching attack is about to be unleashed, and how best to counter it with a defensive front kick.

### Front Kick versus a Punching Attack

When defending against a punching attack with the defensive front kick, your primary target points are your opponent's inner shoulder, his solar plexus, and the underside of his jaw. A front kick to any one of these three regions will instantly stop the attacker's punch. Since each type of punch has its own characteristics, the target of your defensive front kick will vary by the type of attack that is unleashed.

### Front Kick to the Inner Shoulder

The design of the roundhouse punch is that it swings circularly out, and then in toward its target—generally it will be guided toward your head. This punch opens up the body and inner shoulder region of your opponent for a counterattack. Therefore, when a roundhouse punch is launched at you, it can be easily intercepted by delivering a front kick to your opponent's forward shoulder.

By front kicking to your attacker's shoulder, you not only immediately stop the progress of his punch, but you send him back, knocked off balance, as well. As your opponent's offensive technique has been powerfully interrupted and he is off balance, he is in a vulnerable position to be hit by a successful secondary attack. This may ideally allow you to continue forward and forcefully side-kick him to the face.

### Front Kick to the Solar Plexus

The second optimum strike point for the defensive front kick is your opponent's solar plexus. Kicking this target intercepts the oncoming roundhouse punch as well as the straight punch. The solar plexus is a vulnerable and sensitive region on the body. Not only does a strike to this location take less exact targeting than the shoulder strike, but a well-delivered front kick also effortlessly sends your opponent back, possibly to the ground, where, once again, a secondary attack can easily be delivered.

The three front-kick targets against a punching attack are:

☞ the inner shoulder

☞ the solar plexus

☞ the jaw

### Front Kick to the Jaw

The third and final front-kick target, against a punching attack, is the base of your opponent's jaw. The front kick under the jaw not only immediately halts a punching attack, but also knocks your adversary's head directly backward, due to the force and power of the kick. This will leave him completely unable to continue the attack, and no further counterstrikes will be necessary.

# The Side Kick

The basic taekwondo side kick, *yup chagi*, is performed by initially shifting 75 percent of your body weight to your forward base leg as your rear striking leg rises up with a bent knee to waist level. As your striking leg rises, you pivot on the ball of your base foot 180 degrees, and the hip of your striking leg turns toward its target (see Figure 12-3a). Your body leans sideways toward the ground as your striking leg is extended toward your target (see Figure 12-3b). Impact is made with the heel or outside ridge of your foot.

Figure 12-3a: The side kick, Part 1

Figure 12-3b: The side kick, Part 2

## Limitations of the Basic Side Kick

The basic side kick is launched from the rear leg. This makes it very slow and very obvious in combat situations. A trained opponent can easily see it coming and jam or block your kick before you can make contact with it. For this reason, the basic side kick is not a viable technique for self-defense. With a few minor alterations, however, the side kick becomes a very effective weapon in your self-defense arsenal.

## The Momentum-Driven Side Kick

You can substantially increase the range of a kicking technique simply by allowing the momentum of its launch to drive you forward. This is also the case with the side kick.

To experience how this works, visualize a target several feet in front of you.

Enter into a fighting stance and begin by launching the side kick from the rear leg, in the traditional fashion. As you do so, this time, allow your base leg to free itself up and not be firmly anchored to the ground.

By performing the side kick in this fashion, you allow your base leg to slide slightly forward across the floor, propelled by the momentum developed when your rear striking leg is powerfully launched in toward its target. This not only adds range to the traditional side kick but increases its power as well, because the force of your entire body is behind it.

### Mistakes of the Momentum–Driven Side Kick

One of the main problems with delivering the momentum-driven side kick is that many people release the kick's power before they are in range of their target. When performing the side kick in this style, it is imperative to remember not to unleash your striking leg's power from your hip, until your target is close and you are sure of making contact with it.

The power of a side kick comes from the snapping out of your striking leg, at hip level and then at knee level. If this is done too far from your target, the most you can hope to accomplish is that your extended leg will make touching contact with your opponent. You will not, however, have any debilitating impact. Therefore, keep your side kick retracted until target impact is ensured.

## The Lead-Leg Side Kick

The lead-leg side kick is one of the most effective weapons in your offensive and defensive kicking arsenal. It is performed simply by raising your lead leg up to hip level and then unleashing your leg in side-kick fashion from right where you are.

The ideal targets for the lead-leg side kick are your opponent's shin, knee, midsection, and—for more advanced practitioners—face.

The four lead-leg side-kick targets are:
- shin
- knee
- midsection
- face

### Intercepting Defense with a Lead-Leg Side Kick

Suppose an attacker rushes in at you with aggressive intentions. By side-kicking him to the middle-body region with your lead leg, you will immediately stop his attack, and deliver a powerful strike to his ribs. You can continue forward with additional self-defense, as necessary.

### Intercepting the Kick

The lead-leg side kick is an ideal weapon for intercepting your opponent's kicks before they can be fully launched. Your attacker attempts to kick at you. You immediately launch a lead-leg side kick to the ankle region of his striking leg. His kick is immediately held in check, and his body is thrown off balance. This is the ideal time to launch a secondary lead-leg side kick, as he will be unprepared to deal with its onslaught.

The secondary lead-leg side kick is accomplished by simply retracting your striking leg, while keeping it raised, and then immediately redirecting it to a secondary strike location such as the attacker's midsection or face. With this style of rapid, multiple-kick defense, you can achieve victory over an attacker very quickly, without expending much energy.

### Side-Kick Defense Against the Punch

The lead-leg side kick is a very effective initial defense against a punching assault. Since the leg is generally much longer than the arm, simply by delivering a lead-leg side kick to the midsection of a punching opponent, you will instantly stop his punch. Furthermore, he will be left in a vulnerable position for a secondary counterattack.

Figure 12-4: Forward side kick

## The Forward Side Kick

Throughout the history of taekwondo, fighting techniques have continued to be reevaluated and modified to accommodate the ever-growing understanding of body dynamics and combat. An ideal example of this is the changes that have resulted from taekwondo's acceptance as an Olympic sport. Now that the emphasis of the art is no longer placed solely on self-defense, some of its techniques have been modified to increase speed, as opposed to power. This is the case with the forward side kick.

As discussed, the traditional side kick is slow, and a trained opponent can see it coming. To put an end to this problem, the taekwondo side kick has been redesigned.

To launch the taekwondo forward side kick, first bring your kicking leg up in front-kick fashion. You then pivot on the ball of your base foot, while turning your striking leg to reveal the side kick. Your body remains in a forward position, instead of turning to the side.

Although the power of the kick is somewhat diminished by this technique, its speed is increased multifold, because all of the unnecessary movements have been removed from the kicking process. Thus, the forward side kick is substantially more linear, and much more difficult to defend against, than the traditional side kick.

Since the forward side kick is not an extremely powerful weapon, it is used in true combat situations mostly to distract an opponent. This distraction paves the way for you to launch a more debilitating attack.

Figure 12-5: Ground-fighting side kick

## Ground-Fighting Side Kick

If you find yourself looking up from the ground at your attacker, a side kick is one of the best defensive countermeasures you can unleash. To achieve this, brace both of your hands on the ground to reinforce your position. Raise yourself up slightly, by pushing against the ground. Retract your striking leg at hip level. Then, unleash a powerful side kick to your attacker's knee or midsection. This kicking technique can be performed multiple times, if necessary.

## The Roundhouse Kick

The traditional roundhouse kick, *dollo chagi*, is launched from your rear leg (Figure 12-6a). It is directed in a circular fashion from its point of origin to its target. This movement is accomplished by pivoting 180 degrees on the ball of the foot of your base leg, as the kick continues to travel toward its target (Figure 12-6b).

Figure 12-6a: Roundhouse kick, Part 1

Figure 12-6b: Roundhouse kick, Part 2

Impact with the roundhouse kick is made with the instep of your foot, and is ideally directed toward your opponent's knee, thigh, midsection, or—by an advanced practitioner—head.

> The roundhouse kick is a muscle- and momentum-driven weapon. Power is added to it with the snapping out of your knee, just before the kick has reached its impact point.

## Disadvantage of the Traditional Roundhouse Kick

Although the traditional roundhouse kick is very powerful, the leading disadvantage to this kick is that its movement is very obvious. Thus, a trained opponent can easily see it coming and successfully defend against it.

### The Lead-Leg Roundhouse Kick

An effective option to the traditional roundhouse kick is to launch it from your forward leg. When the roundhouse kick is implemented from this position, its technique is virtually the same, but it becomes much harder to block. This is the result of two factors—(1) it is much faster, and (2) it is harder for your opponent to see.

> **B**y launching your roundhouse kick from your forward leg, you can move faster and make it harder for your opponent to see.

### The Low Roundhouse Kick

The low roundhouse kick is an extremely effective offensive weapon to use at the outset of any confrontation. This kick can be rapidly delivered to the outside of your opponent's knee or to his thigh.

When you strike to his knee, your opponent will be thrown off balance—perhaps to such a degree that he will be knocked to the ground. If your impact is not that substantial, you can unleash additional offensive techniques while he is off balance.

If your low-level roundhouse kick is directed toward an adversary's outer thigh, this impact should be used as a prelude to a secondary offensive technique. Although an outer-thigh strike will not immediately disable your opponent, you can nonetheless use this technique to distract him, while you prepare to deliver a powerful secondary attack.

### The Defensive Roundhouse Kick

The roundhouse kick is not an ideal defensive weapon. It can, however, be very effectively used at the outset of a confrontation.

Suppose you have faced off with an opponent. By delivering a powerful lead-leg roundhouse kick to his head before he can unleash a punch, you will gain a substantial advantage over him, and may find that you have already won.

# The Axe Kick

The axe kick, *nerya chagi*, is a close-contact offensive and defensive weapon. The axe kick is performed by rapidly raising your rear, striking leg, in a linear fashion (Figure 12-7a), and then powerfully bringing your heel down onto the shoulder of your opponent (Figure 12-7b). The impact of this kick delivers a devastating blow—often breaking the opponent's shoulder.

## The Defensive Axe Kick

As a defensive weapon, the axe kick can be very effective. For example, suppose a punch has been launched at you—you deflect it, with an in-to-out block. Immediately, you grab hold of your opponent's punching arm, holding him in

Figure 12-7a: Axe kick, Part 1

Figure 12-7b: Axe kick, Part 2

place. You simultaneously bring your axe kick up and strike him on the shoulder with it.

## Extending the Range of the Axe Kick

The basic axe kick is only effective in close-contact infighting situations, but it is quite easy to extend the range of this kick. Enter into a fighting stance and prepare to launch an axe kick from your rear leg. Now, instead of performing it with your base leg locked into position, visualize a target several feet in front of you. Rapidly lift your striking leg. As you do, allow the axe kick's momentum to drag your base foot forward, sliding along the floor, toward your target. You will immediately notice that this is the same base-foot-sliding technique that defined the momentum-driven front kick, and it works in the same way with the axe kick. Although you obviously cannot gain the distance achieved with the momentum-driven front kick, you can move substantially closer toward your opponent, nonetheless.

The axe kick is an ideal infighting weapon when you can be sure that your opponent will remain in close contact. If he moves even slightly, your axe kick will miss its intended target. You can keep him in place by grabbing hold of his clothing and holding him there while you execute this kicking technique.

## The Out-to-In Axe Kick

The traditional axe kick is brought inward, across your body, and then downward onto its target. The out-to-in axe kick is swung outward and is then brought down onto your adversary's shoulder.

The out-to-in axe kick is also a close-contact infighting weapon. It can most effectively be dispatched when your attacker has taken hold of your clothing, or you have hold of his. Then, the kick is rapidly brought up and delivered to his shoulder region.

### Axe Kick Precautions

The axe kick is a very powerful weapon. For this reason, it must be executed with utmost caution whenever you practice it with a training partner. Remember, striking an opponent with this kick can easily break his collarbone or shoulder bone. Even in the most casual of circumstances, this kick is very dangerous.

## The Hook Kick

The basic hook kick, *gullgi chagi*, is launched from your rear leg. You pivot approximately 180 degrees on your base foot as your striking leg travels forward across the front of your body (Figure 12-8a). Your striking leg is simultaneously brought up, raising it to impact height. The lower part of your striking leg is then powerfully snapped back at knee level, making heel contact with your intended target—which is ideally the head of your opponent (Figure 12-8b).

Figure 12-8a: Hook kick, Part 1    Figure 12-8b: Hook kick, Part 2

## The Lead-Leg Hook Kick

The forward lead-leg hook kick is launched in substantially the same fashion as the rear-leg hook kick. The only difference is that it has less distance to travel and is, therefore, a much more rapid offensive weapon.

## The Offensive Hook Kick

To successfully use the hook kick, you must be in close proximity to your adversary. Unlike the axe kick, it is not a linear technique; you cannot grab hold of your opponent and keep him in place as you unleash it. Therefore, to use this kick as a first-strike offensive weapon, you must deliver it rapidly, at the beginning of a confrontation. After the first few moments, a hook kick is not a viable weapon, because its delivery is limited in range. It will not work if you are too close to or far from your opponent, and its movement is obvious, so it is easy to defend against. Therefore, in its traditional form, the hook kick's primary effectiveness is as a first-strike weapon.

## The Defensive Hook Kick

The hook kick becomes very effective when you use it as a secondary technique, in association with a preliminary defensive kick. For example, suppose your opponent attempts a front kick at you. You jam his technique with a low side kick, then retract your kick and immediately unleash a hook kick to his head. This will instantly disable your opponent.

# Taekwondo's Spinning Kicks

Spinning kicks are highly effective offensive and defensive weapons, because most fights are fought face-to-face. By spinning around to the rear, not only have you realigned the structure of the fight to your own advantage, but you have created the element of surprise, as well.

*The most important factor in executing any spinning kick is to keep your eye on your opponent.*

The most important factor to remember when using any spinning kick is to keep your eye on your opponent. If you do not, he may reposition himself as your technique is being unleashed, and you may find your spin being met with a fist to your face.

Keeping your eye on your opponent is accomplished by pivoting your head before you actually execute any spinning kick. This may sound awkward, and you might think it would give your opponent time to react, but don't worry. Through practice, you will learn to pivot your head so rapidly and naturally that virtually no time elapses between the pivot and the performance of the kick.

If your opponent does move during your spin, you do not have to unleash your intended kick. You can simply continue through with your spinning motion, realign yourself with your opponent, then deliver the appropriate type of assault for the situation.

There are three spinning kicks that are very effective in combat situations: the back kick, the spinning heel kick, and the spinning axe kick. Each of these kicking techniques possesses different advantages, so we will discuss each separately.

> The three spinning kicks that are ideal for combat situations are:
> ☞ the back kick
> ☞ the spinning heel kick
> ☞ the spinning axe kick

## The Back Kick

Structurally similar to the side kick, the back kick (*dwei chagi*) is executed by first turning your head around, thus keeping an eye on your target. This head turning is performed as you simultaneously pivot your body on the ball of the foot of your lead base leg 180 degrees (see Figure 12-9a). Your kicking technique is then launched from rear-leg position—in side-kick fashion (see Figure 12-9b).

The back kick is a muscle-driven technique. Impact with this kick is made with the heel or the outside ridge of your foot (Figure 12-9c). The ideal targets for the back kick are your opponent's knee, midsection, or head.

### Advantage of the Back Kick

The primary offensive and defensive advantage of the back kick is that your back is the only region exposed to your opponent. This allows him little effective space for counterattack.

Figure 12-9a: Back kick, Part 1

Figure 12-9b: Back kick, Part 2

Figure 12-9c: Back kick, Part 3

## The Offensive Back Kick

The back kick is one of the most effective, aggressive offensive techniques in your kicking arsenal. It can be performed as one single offensive movement or in a rapid-fire continuation, from one back kick on to the next and the next. One, two, three, or four of these kicks may be consecutively launched, using your legs alternately. This is an excellent method of continually striking at your opponent.

## The Defensive Back Kick

The back kick is an ideal weapon to counter an attacker's punching technique. Simply launch it to his midsection while his punch is in motion. By doing this, you move his target, most probably your face, out of the path of his punching attack, and deliver a powerful blow to his body.

## The Jumping Back Kick

As you progress in your competence with the back kick, you can move this technique on to the next level and raise it off the ground, with the jumping back kick (*edan dwei chagi*). To accomplish this, slightly bend the knee of your base leg, and then thrust yourself upward as

Figure 12-10a: Jumping back kick, Part 1          Figure 12-10b: Jumping back kick, Part 2

you spin. Raising your body from the ground not only aids you in obtaining higher strike points on your opponent, such as his chest or head, but it also allows you to avoid low-level attacks from the ground, such as low sweep kicks.

### Precaution for the Jumping Back Kick

It is essential that you learn the correct way to raise a kick from its ground position to a jumping position. When performing a jumping back kick, most practitioners use their own exaggerated body momentum and the forced bending of their base knee to achieve the spring needed to raise them off the ground—but this style of performing a jumping back kick alerts your opponent to your intentions. Therefore, it is imperative to make the jumping version of a back kick as effortless as possible. You will have to develop your spring by lowering your base knee only slightly, and this takes dedicated practice. But when you perform a jumping back kick in this way, your opponent will not be alerted to your oncoming technique.

The three back-kick targets are:

☞ knee

☞ midsection

☞ head

## The Spinning Heel Kick

The spinning heel kick, *dui huryo chagi*, is one of the most powerful techniques in a taekwondo practitioner's kicking arsenal. The momentum this

Figure 12-11a: Spinning heel kick, Part 1

Figure 12-11b: Spinning heel kick, Part 2

Figure 12-11c: Spinning heel kick, Part 3

kick can have a devastating effect upon any object it strikes.

The spinning heel kick is executed by turning your head around behind you, to make sure your target has not moved, as you simultaneously pivot 180 degrees on the ball of the foot of your forward leg (see Figure 12-11a). Your rear leg lifts off the ground and proceeds toward its target in a circular fashion (Figure 12-11b). This kick strikes its target with the back of your heel (Figure 12-11c). The spinning heel kick is ideally targeted at the midsection or head of your attacker.

When you deliver the spinning heel kick, it is important to drive your kick "through" your target. That is, do not plan to halt your kick at the target location, but instead allow it to powerfully drive into the target, coming to rest at a much deeper point. This will give your spinning heel kick substantially more power, and make it much more difficult to defend against.

### The Offensive Spinning Heel Kick

The offensive spinning heel kick is most effectively unleashed at the moment your adversary has closed in on you. At the outset of a physical confrontation, your opponent will not be expecting you to rapidly deliver this advanced kicking technique, so he will be open to its assault.

**The Defensive Spinning Heel Kick**

The defensive spinning heel kick is most successfully launched at the moment you have completed a block or a deflection. For example, suppose your opponent punches at you. You block this punch with an in-to-out cross-arm block. Since you are already moving in a circular fashion, you can immediately follow up this block with a spinning heel kick. This will maintain the uninterrupted flow of your circular movement, and you will be able to deliver a devastating blow to your opponent.

## The Spinning Axe Kick

The spinning axe kick is a highly valuable combative technique. It can penetrate your opponent's defenses and defeat him in a single strike.

As with the basic axe kick, the spinning axe kick is very dangerous. When performing this kick, you are not only targeting your opponent's shoulder, but adding momentum-driven spinning power to your kicking technique. For this reason, in training and friendly sparring sessions, you must be extremely careful when using this advanced kicking technique.

Taekwondo's arsenal of kicks provides you with a vast number of variations on its techniques, to allow you to tailor any kick to fit different confrontational situations.

To execute the spinning axe kick, you pivot your head and body around behind you. Your striking leg rises up vertically. You then bring your heel powerfully down onto your adversary's shoulder.

# Taekwondo's Stepping Kicks

Taekwondo's stepping kicks add distance and power to many of the art's basic kicking techniques. By adding a stepping element to your kicks, you can readily move in on an opponent in a very aggressive fashion and immediately take control of the confrontation.

## The Stepping Side Kick

The stepping side kick is one of the most powerful kicks in the taekwondo practitioner's combat arsenal. It is performed by rapidly placing your base leg

Figure 12-12a: Stepping side kick, Part 1

Figure 12-12b: Stepping side kick, Part 2

Figure 12-12c: Stepping side kick, Part 3

behind your striking leg (see Figure 12-12a). This provides you with added distance and substantially increases the kick's momentum-driven power. The striking leg is then raised and powerfully extended out, in side-kick fashion (Figures 12-12b and 12-12c).

As an offensive weapon, the stepping side kick rapidly penetrates your opponent's defenses. You face off with your adversary, immediately deliver a stepping side kick under his guard, and he will be sent backward to the ground.

This is a kick designed to injure any target that it strikes. As such, it is an ideal weapon to launch as a beginning technique in competition or in street altercations. Not only is the stepping side kick a rapid and powerful kick, but defending against its onslaught is quite difficult. The only option your opponent may have, to defend himself, is to rapidly retreat from its attack. If this occurs, you simply continue through with an additional step behind your striking leg, giving you more distance, and then unleash the power of this kick.

## The Stepping Roundhouse Kick

The stepping roundhouse kick is delivered in a similar fashion to the stepping side kick. You ready yourself in a fighting stance. You then place your rear leg behind your lead leg, giving you added distance. Once this has been done, you powerfully deliver a targeted roundhouse kick from your lead leg.

The stepping roundhouse kick is a very rapid and powerful kicking technique. It is used to close the distance on your opponent and rapidly deliver a first strike to such targets as the midsection or the side of the head.

## The Stepping Axe Kick

Another stepping kick that will allow you to rapidly close the distance between you and your opponent is the stepping axe kick. To perform this technique, ready yourself in a fighting stance. When it is time for you to move in toward your target, rapidly place your rear foot behind your forward striking leg, stepping in deeply toward your objective. As your rear leg steps behind your forward leg, simultaneously rapidly raise your front leg up in axe-kick fashion. Once the desired distance has been gained, powerfully drive your kicking leg down through your target.

By performing the stepping axe kick, you can cross great distances and pursue your opponent, while still maintaining your balance and protecting your upper body from attack, with your arms. The stepping axe kick is not only an extremely penetrating offensive weapon, but it is also very difficult to defend against.

## The Stepping Hook Kick

As with the previously described stepping kicks, you can also add enormous range to the hook kick by adding the stepping motion to it. Whereas the basic hook kick is very range-limited, the stepping hook kick is a very effective first strike offensive weapon, because you can rapidly move in on your opponent and kick him in the head with a maneuver that is very difficult to defend against.

To perform the stepping hook kick, begin in a fighting stance. Rapidly place your rear leg behind your lead leg. As you do so, bring your striking leg up and unleash a hook kick.

# Taekwondo's Jumping Kicks

Jumping kicks are generally very impressive to watch in demonstrations and in the movies. In a confrontational situation, however, anyone who jumps off the ground to attack an opponent is left open to countless forms of defense. Furthermore, none of the forms of defense would have been encountered if the practitioner had kept his or her feet on the ground.

For this reason, elaborate jumping kicks are never used in taekwondo combat—they are just too easy to defend against. Nonetheless, taekwondo possesses an arsenal of jumping kicks, each of which have been revised and designed to be an effective tool of defense and a viable weapon of combat.

In order for it to be a successful form of attack or counterattack, a jumping kick must be very easy to perform and must travel to its target in a very rapid manner.

## The Jumping Front Kick

The jumping front kick, *edan ap chagi*, is generally the first offensive jumping kick a taekwondo student is taught. The jumping front kick is traditionally launched by beginning in a fighting stance and then snapping the rear leg forward and up, in order to gain enough momentum to lift the body from the ground. This allows the other leg to snap forward in the air, in front-kick fashion. Although this is the accepted method of delivering this jumping kick, performing it in this way poses many problems, if you are trying to launch an attack.

### Problems with the Traditional Jumping Front Kick

The jumping front kick, when delivered in a traditional fashion, is not only a very obvious kicking technique, but a very slow one, as well. The reason the traditional jumping front kick is so obvious and slow is that the rear, non-kicking leg is launched first and directs the kick upward and forward. This makes the kick very easy for a competent opponent to defend against.

The traditional jumping front kick is designed to ideally target upward strike locations, such as under an opponent's jaw. Because it follows this upward path, this kick has an extremely limited range of distance and target area.

Once the traditional jumping front kick has been launched, it is very difficult to redirect its path or implementation. A trained opponent can easily see it coming, and he only needs to sidestep its path of assault to make the kick miss. He can then easily deliver a counterstrike.

## Redefining the Jumping Front Kick

As you have previously learned, the basic front kick is a very simple, linear technique. It possesses no excess movement, only very direct targeting applications. This is the reason it is so fast and so effective in physical combat. If you take the simple approach of the basic front kick and apply its structure to a jumping kick, you will then be able to develop a jumping front kick that is not only very fast, but difficult to defend against.

Begin to redevelop your jumping front kick by entering into a fighting stance. Visualize an imaginary target in front of you, or locate yourself in front of a hanging bag. Launch a basic front kick from your rear leg. Feel how simply and easily this kicking technique is achieved. Now, stand back a little farther from your target and perform the momentum-driven front kick. As previously detailed in this chapter, allow the power of your rear leg to move your base leg along the floor. Again, mentally observe how easily this kicking technique was unleashed.

Figure 12-13a: Redefined jumping front kick, Part 1

To take the front kick to the level of a very effective jumping technique, you only need to allow this same power and momentum to drive you upward. To achieve this, locate yourself in front of your target. Ready yourself in a fighting stance. Just as you are about to launch this front kick, allow the knee of your base leg to bend down very slightly (see Figure 12-13a). Now, kick your rear leg powerfully forward in front-kick

Figure 12-13b: Redefined jumping front kick, Part 2

Figure 12-13c: Redefined jumping front kick, Part 3

fashion. As you do this, simultaneously allow your slightly bent base leg to launch you upward, off the ground (Figure 12-13b). Allow the momentum of this technique to drive you deeply in, forward, toward your target (Figure 12-13c).

What you have achieved is a jumping front kick that does not rely on both legs to give you the momentum to raise your body off the ground. By doing this, you have not only simplified the jumping front kick technique, but you have made it substantially faster and much harder to defend against, as well.

As with other taekwondo kicks previously described, it is very important to remember, whenever you perform a jumping front kick, never to completely snap out the lower section of your striking leg until you are sure of striking your target. If you snap your kick out before your target is in range, you will expend the force of the kick too early and fail to make powerful contact with your opponent.

### The Offensive Jumping Front Kick

This style of jumping front kick makes it quite easy to drive in deeply toward an opponent and strike either his midsection or his face. It also reduces your opponent's chances to rapidly retreat, since you are on top of him before he can read your oncoming offensive moves. If, in fact, he does successfully move backward or sidestep your attack, you can land balanced and enter into a secondary fighting technique very easily. Thus, you will not be unnecessarily bound to only one offensive maneuver.

The redefined jumping front kick is an ideal first-strike weapon against an opponent in competition, because you can rapidly move in on him. It is additionally a very powerful self-defense weapon. For example, suppose your opponent unleashes a roundhouse kick or spinning heel kick toward you. If you quickly lean back out of its path, the kick will miss—and the moment it misses is the ideal opportunity to launch a powerful jumping front kick. By

Figure 12-14a: Jumping side kick, Part 1

Figure 12-14b: Jumping side kick, Part 2

doing this, you will immediately make striking contact with your opponent and take control of the competition.

## The Jumping Side Kick

The jumping side kick, *edan yup chagi*, is performed by beginning in a fighting stance. Your rear leg steps forward as a means to propel your body off the ground (see Figure 12-14a). Your rear striking leg is then sent forward, toward your target, in side-kick fashion (Figure 12-14b).

### Redefining the Jumping Side Kick

The jumping side kick is a very powerful and extremely effective technique for rapidly moving in on an opponent and striking him with debilitating force. Although this kick is very effective, there are some crucial elements many people overlook. The biggest mistake the novice taekwondo practitioner makes when unleashing a jumping side kick is extending the striking leg the moment he or she is in the air. If you do this, you may strike your opponent, but your strike will not have a substantial impact. Therefore, it is essential, when you are unleashing this technique, to keep your striking leg retracted and never extend it until you are in close proximity to your target. At the point when you are about to encounter your target, rapidly extend your leg and strike with force. In this way, your opponent will be hit with substantially more power.

The second mistake many people make, when unleashing a jumping side kick, is to attempt to strike at their opponent's head. If you make facial contact with this technique, the effect on your opponent can be devastating. The problem, however, is that the head is a much smaller target than the body. Therefore, a trained opponent, who can easily see this style of offensive kick being unleashed, can quickly move his head out of

> In order to perform an effective jumping side kick, extend your striking leg only when you are in close proximity to your target.

its path of attack. If, however, you are targeting your opponent's body, you will have a much larger target area, and a much greater chance of making impact.

# Knee Fighting

Close-contact fighting has always proven to be one of the most complicated situations for taekwondo practitioners. Although most of taekwondo's offensive and defensive techniques are developed to be used when you are a few feet away from your opponent, there is one technique that is ideally suited to infighting: knee fighting, or *mooreup*.

Although knee strikes are not used in taekwondo competition, they are an essential element of taekwondo self-defense. Therefore, you must develop the ability to unleash a correct knee strike.

## Infighting

In close proximity, your available striking techniques become very limited, which is why it is difficult to rapidly and successfully defend yourself once your opponent has moved in on you, and possibly taken hold of your clothing. First of all, there is not enough distance between your body and your opponent's for you to effectively kick him. And, with the exception of the uppercut punch, your punching defense is limited to wildly thrown roundhouse punches. Therefore, the taekwondo knee strike is an essential weapon. The knee strike makes an excellent close-contact fighting tool because it doesn't require much space to make its attack effective.

## Understanding the Knee Strike

The knee strike takes little advanced training to perform. There are, however, certain limitations to this technique. Therefore, you must fully explore the science of knee fighting, to learn what not to do, before you can understand what the knee can effectively accomplish.

The knee is one of the most sensitive joints on the human body. It is quite easily damaged. When you strike with the knee, it is very important to do it correctly; otherwise, you run the risk of injuring your knee instead of defending yourself successfully.

Knee fighting is the only effective technique for combat when your opponent is only a few feet away.

Your knee should always be bent when you attack with it. By bending your knee, you not only isolate its impact point but you keep it from bending back unnaturally, which can tear your ligaments and cartilage—or in more severe cases can break your kneecap.

A knee strike should never be delivered in a side-to-side format. That is, never attempt to strike with the side of your knee. The side area of your knee joint is very sensitive, and your lower leg can easily be twisted away from your upper leg if you attempt to strike with your knee in this way.

The part of your knee that should be used as a striking weapon is the upper part. Reach down to your thigh and follow your upper leg muscle to the point where it meets the kneecap. This is the ideal strike point for knee attacks.

A proper knee strike is accomplished by rapidly lifting your knee up and into its target. The power of the knee strike is initiated at the hip, and is driven forward with the muscles of the upper leg.

## Knee Strikes

The first strike point most people think of when utilizing a knee attack is the opponent's groin. This is, in fact, a very good location to aim for, especially if your opponent has grabbed you in a forward choke hold or similar frontal attack. In this type of attack, your opponent's groin region is easily accessible, and a powerful knee strike can make instantaneous contact and lead you to victory in the confrontation.

Although the knee can strike virtually any location on your opponent's body, given the right set of circumstances, there are several locations that are ideal knee-strike targets: the groin, the ribs, the kidneys, and—for the advanced practitioner—the underside of the opponent's jaw. The time to strike at these various targets is determined only by the type of encounter in which you find yourself.

One of the most important things to remember, when using the knee as a weapon, is that you should never use your knee to strike at a location on your opponent's body that you must travel to reach. That is, like the various punching techniques and many of the traditional martial art kicks, the knee strike is not an ideal long-distance weapon. The very elements that make the knee an ideal close-contact weapon make it inefficient in distant applications.

If you attempt to launch yourself in toward your opponent, with the momentum you can gain from jumping off your non–knee-striking leg, you not only leave yourself off balance, but you also open and expose your body to powerful counterattacks. Therefore, the use of the knee as a striking weapon should be limited to close-quarter infighting.

The choice of a knee strike is determined by two factors:

☞ Is the target easily reachable?

☞ Will a knee strike have a sufficiently debilitating effect on your opponent?

If the answer to both of these questions is yes, then that is the time to perform a powerful knee strike.

# part 4
## conditioning

**U**NDERSTANDING how to perform the physical movements of taekwondo—whether they are kicks, punches, or blocks— is only the first step in your immersion in the art. Taekwondo is much more than simply a martial art that teaches physical combat. Taekwondo teaches methods for taking your body to a level of mind/body coordination never experienced by the average person. To this end, as a taekwondo practitioner, you may wish to add additional training tools to your overall workout regimen. From this, you will gain a new sense of physical and mental advancement.

# chapter 13
# stretching

**S**TRETCHING is an exercise that causes your muscles to increase in flexibility. As enhanced flexibility is essential to your overall performance in taekwondo, stretching is a prerequisite for all taekwondo training sessions.

Stretching is a progressive exercise. As such, the more often you stretch the more elastic your muscles become.

## Understanding Stretching

*S*tretching before you work out helps your body remain free from muscle-tear injuries. Stretching also prepares your body for the rigors of the workout ahead by increasing muscle elasticity and increasing blood flow through your veins.

As the years have progressed and the study of physiology has given us a new understanding of the human body, one of the things we have learned is that you should never stretch a sedentary muscle. That is, do not jump out of bed in the morning, or out of a chair you have been sitting in for several hours, and immediately begin stretching. Instead, you must invigorate your body before you stretch. This process can be as easy as shaking part of your body for a few minutes to cause additional blood circulation. You can continue this process by rubbing the area you are planning to stretch—additionally providing enhanced circulation. Of course, if you have the available space, a few jumping jacks quickly invigorate your body.

Always begin stretching slowly. Allow your muscles to become accustomed to the process before you attempt to perform a deep stretch.

When you begin your initial stretching, never force it. You do not want to bounce into your stretch, causing your own weight to make you go deeper into a stretch. Although this is a common practice, it can actually damage your muscles. Therefore, whatever stretch you are performing, allow you body to naturally progress into it.

## Taekwondo and Stretching

All stretching exercises are good to perform in association with taekwondo training. For taekwondo, you want every area of your body to become supple and elastic. Although all stretches are good for taekwondo, there are a few basic movements that are commonly performed as part of a taekwondo warmup.

Figure 13-1: Side and back stretch

Figure 13-2: Forward stretch

### The Side and Back Stretch

To do the side and back stretch, you stand in a natural posture with your feet approximately one shoulders' width apart. You bring one of your arms out and over your head. This causes you to lean to one side (see Figure 13-1).

This is an ideal warmup exercise that stretches your lower back, side, upper body, shoulder, and arm muscles. You should perform this stretch at least three times on each side, for one minute each, prior to stretching other parts of your body.

### The Forward Stretch

For the forward stretch, you separate your legs at a greater than shoulders' width distance. You then lean forward, touching your hands to the floor (see Figure 13-2).

This stretch loosens your lower back and rear leg muscles. It should be performed at least three times, for one minute each, prior to moving on to other stretching exercises.

### The Seated Forward Stretch

For the seated forward stretch, you sit down on the ground. You bend your knee and

Figure 13-3: Seated forward stretch

Figure 13-4: Side leg stretch

place the foot of your nonstretching leg against the inner thigh of your stretching leg—which is extended in front of you. You lean down over your stretching leg, attempting to touch your foot (see Figure 13-3).

This stretch is ideal to loosen up your lower and middle back. It is also an excellent stretch to loosen up your rear leg muscles for kicking.

This stretching exercise should be performed from three to five times, for one minute each, prior to training.

**The Side Leg Stretch**

For the side leg stretch, you begin in a standing position. When you are ready to stretch, you bend one of your knees and let the weight of your body sink down on that side, until it rests on the ball of the foot. Your stretching leg is extended (see Figure 13-4).

This is a great stretch for your leg muscles. It can be performed for up to five repetitions of one minute each.

A simple exercise to perform, if you wish to stretch your legs in the morning or after a long period of sitting, is to elevate your heels off the ground. This is accomplished by rising up on the balls of your feet and then lowering yourself, several times. This simple exercise will quickly cause additional blood flow through your legs, and you will be ready for stretching.

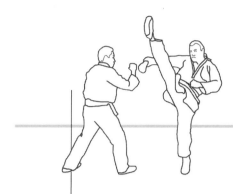

# chapter 14
# taekwondo and cardioaerobic conditioning

FOR THE AVERAGE PERSON, taekwondo is a great method of working out. Not only does it increase endurance and stamina, but it teaches the practitioner new methods of self-defense—while providing a great cardiovascular workout. In and of itself, taekwondo is an excellent source of cardioaerobic conditioning. In every class, students are led through a series of exercises that increases their heart rate and provides a healthy workout.

For the average sedentary individual, taekwondo may be all that is needed to begin to embrace a new, healthier and more active lifestyle. But is taekwondo enough for cardiovascular fitness?

No doubt, when most people begin to study taekwondo, the workout will truly push their bodies to physical levels never before experienced. After a period of time, however, the students will commonly become accustomed to the training and will subconsciously learn how to pace themselves throughout the workout. Because of this fact, the workout will not be as intense.

Though taekwondo provides a healthy workout, complementary cardioaerobic training will help to develop endurance, stamina, and overall physical conditioning.

There is one part of a taekwondo class that normally makes practitioners realize whether or not they need to add additional cardioaerobic training to their regimen. That part of the class is sparring.

Although you can pace yourself throughout the normal class workout, when it comes to sparring, there is little you can do to control the match. This is particularly true when you come up against a very aggressive opponent. In these cases, you are oftentimes pushed to your physical limits. This is the point when a practitioner commonly decides if additional cardioaerobic conditioning should be added to his or her workout schedule.

Cardioaerobic training has been a mainstay of virtually all athletes, from every discipline. This is also the case with taekwondo. But what is the right program to add to taekwondo training, to enhance endurance, stamina, and overall physical condition?

# Running and Taekwondo

There are few activities that are as directly linked to cardiovascular fitness as running. It is an ideal activity to add to your taekwondo training regimen. Running not only develops bodily endurance, but it develops additional leg strength as well.

Running is the ideal complement to your taekwondo training because it enhances endurance and develops leg strength.

Running is an individual activity. As such, it allows you to control how far or how fast you will run.

## Beginning to Run

Just as stretching is essential to taekwondo training, it is also essential to running. Therefore, before you run, you must stretch to loosen up your muscles, in order to avoid unnecessary injury.

After you have stretched, you must warm up your body before you run. An ideal way to do this is to begin to walk at a fast pace for several hundred yards. Once your body is warmed up, and you feel you are ready, you may begin your run.

Depending on your current physical condition, an ideal distance to set as a goal for your initial run is half a mile. To those who have never run, this may seem like an enormous distance, but, in fact, it is not. It can be comfortably run in approximately fifteen minutes.

To the more seasoned athlete, a half mile may seem like much too short a distance, but for those who have not previously run, it is a good distance to set as a training goal.

When you begin to run, you do not want to overexert yourself or strain your body. For this reason, even if you can push yourself to run much farther than half a mile, it is not a good idea to do so at the outset. Instead, let your body become accustomed to running for a few days before you begin to extend your distance.

Once your body begins to feel natural while running, you can begin to run for longer periods of time and for extended distances. If you are running on a treadmill, it is easy to gauge the distance of the walking and the running portions of your workout. If you are running on a track, tell yourself that after a certain number of days, perhaps three, you will extend your run by one lap. If you are running on the beach, you can gauge your run by lifeguard stations, as they are set one-quarter of a mile apart. At the appropriate time, decide to run to the next station. If you are running in your neighborhood, push yourself to run one additional block after a few days of training.

The reason for running is to build up your endurance. You will, therefore, want to continually push yourself to run for extended periods of time and for extended distances. For the average taekwondo practitioner, a maximum of four miles is a common goal. By achieving this distance, you will be running for approximately thirty to forty-five minutes. This is plenty of time for your body to gain the cardiovascular workout needed and to send you to the next level of physical fitness.

## The Boxer's Run

For those taekwondo practitioners who are running to enhance their endurance for competition, a training method used by boxers may be employed. Boxers will jog for a prescribed distance or period of time—most commonly, one mile or ten minutes. Then, they will sprint for three minutes. As soon

> The boxer's run consists of alternating between running and sprinting and is an ideal method of endurance training.

as the three minutes are over, they will return to a jog. They will again jog for one mile and then begin the three-minute sprint. The reason for the three-minute sprint is that this is the length of a boxing round.

Anyone who has sparred a round during taekwondo training knows that a three-minute round can drain all of your energy. For this reason, your stamina must be so developed that you can perform at a level of excellence during the three-minute round, rest for a few moments, and then come back and give it your all for a second and a third time. The boxer's run is an ideal method to develop this level of endurance.

### Sprint Precautions

When it is done correctly, sprint training is a great way to build up your endurance. The mistake many people make, however, is taking up sprinting before they have trained in distance-oriented endurance running. They sprint for a short distance and then walk for a few minutes. Once they have cooled down, they sprint again.

This style of running is not a beneficial form of endurance training. When you train in this manner, you rapidly and unnaturally accelerate your heart rate, and then you allow it to slow down, only to be immediately accelerated again once you have regained your breath. For this reason, sprint training should only be undertaken once you can comfortably run for four miles. Then, it should only be performed once you have become acutely aware of your body's reaction to running—because you will want to stop this advanced endurance training if you find that it is causing any physical problems.

## The Cool-Down

Once you have completed your run, what is known as a cool-down (also called a warm-down) is an absolute necessity. You must never finish a run and then immediately get into your car and drive home, or just stop and sit down. This can cause your muscles to cramp.

An ideal activity to perform as a cool-down after you run is to slowly bring your run to a conclusion and then continue to walk for a quarter mile. Walking allows your heart rate to slow down and your body to cool down in a natural manner.

Once your cool-down is complete, stretching is also an absolute necessity. Running develops leg muscles. As a taekwondo practitioner, you must keep your legs loose and limber to perform the kicking techniques, so take several minutes to stretch at the end of your cool-down.

### *Running Precautions*

Running is a great source of cardioaerobic fitness. There is a downside to it, however. Running can be very damaging to your ankle, knee, and hip joints, and can cause problems with the bones of your feet.

Running on cement is known to pose the biggest problems for a runner's body. Cement is a very dense compound. With every stride, this unyielding surface has a hard impact on your feet, which greatly increases the potential for injury.

If you do not wish to purchase a treadmill, or if you do not have access to a gym that provides them, running on a high school or college track is a good alternative to running on cement. Most schools open their tracks to the public in the afternoon.

Although running on the beach provides a very giving surface for your run, there are also problems with this environment. Sand possesses little consistency, which means that you may be running along and your foot will sink into a deep crevasse. This can cause foot, ankle, or knee injury.

Where you decide to run must be your decision. Wherever you run, it is essential that you pay attention to sprains, joint pain, or muscle pulls, as these seemingly minor injuries can have long-term effects.

Monitor your body carefully. If you are encountering pain, take a few days off and let your body heal.

## Bicycling and Taekwondo

Another great form of endurance training is bicycling. Bicycling is much less damaging to the joints of your legs than running. For this reason, many taekwondo practitioners choose this means of endurance training.

*Bicycling is another great addition to your taekwondo training— it develops endurance and is less damaging on your joints than running.*

To add bicycling to your training, you begin in much the same manner as you do for running. You must always begin by stretching to loosen up your muscles and help to prevent muscle-tear injuries. Once your stretching is complete, you will need a warmup period. In the case of bicycling, this may be riding for a few blocks in a slow and natural pattern.

Once you have warmed up, you will want to increase your speed of travel. As with running, you can go as fast or as slow as you are comfortable with— whatever feels most natural for you.

You will want to set an initial distance goal for your bicycle ride. While bicycling, you can easily cover one mile or more without becoming fatigued. So, one mile to your destination and one mile returning is a good beginning target.

As your endurance grows and you become more comfortable with bicycling, you will want to increase your distance. In the case of bicycling, twenty miles per training session may be your final objective.

## Bicycle Sprints

You may wish to eventually add sprints to your bicycling program. These sprints can go on for three minutes, as in the boxer's run, or can be extended to a longer period of time, according to your level of endurance.

As with running, you should not tire yourself out, while sprinting, to the degree that you must stop and catch your breath. Simply slow down your pace when you've gone the appropriate time or distance, and continue to your destination.

You may want to sprint for three minutes, go back to a normal pedalling pace for a mile, and then return to a sprint. Once you have achieved a high enough level of endurance, you may wish to add bicycle sprints at four or five intervals during your ride.

Virtually all modern gyms have computerized stationary bicycles that allow you to set your desired distance, your sprint intervals, and your cool-down level. So it is not necessary to purchase a bicycle if you wish to add bicycle riding to your overall taekwondo endurance training

## Cooling Down

Cooling down is just as necessary with bike riding as it is with running. Cooling down on a bike ride is, in many ways, easier than it is with running. For your cool-down, all you will need to do is to slow your pace as you approach your final destination. You will want to cool down for approximately the final ten minutes of your ride.

Once you have concluded, stretching to loosen up your back and leg muscles is an absolute necessity. You may then move forward into your day.

 ### Bicycle Precautions

Bicycling is not normally as detrimental to your leg joints as running, but there can be problems. This is especially true if you are riding a bicycle that is not correctly fitted to your body, or if your bicycle is not set up correctly.

The rule for choosing the size of the racing-style bicycle, or the single-speed bicycles known as cruisers, is that you should put your leg over the main upper frame bar—the piece of metal that is parallel to the ground. This frame bar should be just below or lightly touching your groin region. For the all-terrain bikes (ATB) or the hybrid bikes, when you stand over the main frame bar, this bar should be approximately three inches below your groin.

Once you have the right size bicycle for you, the next step is to set it up correctly. The most important setting is that of the seat. The height of the seat will directly affect how your knees and hips function while you ride. Therefore, if your seat is not set correctly, you can easily injure your knee or hip joints.

To set your seat height, you must sit on your bicycle. Allow one pedal to be all the way down. Your leg, when it touches this pedal, should be almost straight, with only a slight bend.

Many people feel it is more comfortable to sit low on a bicycle, and their seats are therefore positioned far too low. This is a mistake, especially in regards to long-distance endurance training and the injuries it can cause. If you are going to take up endurance riding, be sure that your bicycle is the right size and set up appropriately for your body.

# Swimming and Taekwondo

Swimming is another great form of endurance training that is commonly added to an individual's taekwondo training program. Unlike running and bicycling, swimming does not pose a risk to the joints of your body. As you will be exercising in a liquid environment, the impact of the training environment, and your body's resistance to it, are substantially reduced.

Prior to swimming you must stretch. Stretching is the essential element of all forms of physical activity. You will also want to warm up. A swimming warmup may consist of performing several jumping jacks or push-ups in order to get your blood flowing and raise your heart rate. In other cases, you may wish to get into the pool and perform a few slow laps with the backstroke or sidestroke, to get your body ready for training.

Swimming is a great cardioaerobic exercise and an excellent way to bring endurance and strength training into your routine.

For swimming, as for all other cardioaerobic activities, you will want to set a beginning goal to get you started on your training program. An ideal goal is from two to four laps, depending on the size of the pool. You will swim this distance with the standard overhand stroke, since this is the most cardioaerobically invigorating.

Do not attempt to be the fastest swimmer in the pool. Simply set a natural pace that is right for you, and stay with it. Swim to the end of the pool, turn around, and swim back.

Many people do not realize that swimming is an extremely cardioaerobic activity. When you first begin to swim, you will become tired and fatigued much more rapidly than you ever imagined. Therefore, it is not a good idea to begin your swimming program in a lake or the ocean, and set some distant point as your target. You may get halfway there and not possess enough energy to go the rest of the way. It is far safer to begin your program in a swimming pool, where you can grab hold of the side and rest, at any time, if the need arises.

With all cardioaerobic activities, the more time you devote to your training, the more rapidly you will become proficient at your chosen sport. Swimming is no different. You will want to set an end goal for swimming. An ideal distance is one mile. Depending on the size of the pool, this can be anywhere up to twenty or more laps.

Developing the ability to swim for one mile will provide you with the needed stamina and endurance to encounter all levels of taekwondo training. It is an ideal form of training to add to a taekwondo regimen, as the benefits are great and the chances of injuries are small.

# Cool-Down

During the swimming cool-down, you are still active, but not pushing yourself as you did with the overhand stroke. An ideal method to cool down is by performing your final lap while swimming in a slow backstroke or sidestroke. This will allow you to catch your breath, and your heart rate to slow down.

Upon the completion of your cool-down, you will want to stretch. Perhaps you can perform a few stretches in the pool—with your head above water, of course! Then get out and finish your stretching.

### Swimming Precautions

As with all other physical activities, you will want to pace yourself while swimming. In running and bicycling, you can stop at any point. In swimming, especially if you are not swimming within the relatively safe confines of a pool, stopping is not always an option.

It is not unusual for leg muscles to cramp up while you swim. If you perform this activity in a large lake or ocean, with no lifeguard, this can be disastrous. As such, if your choice for swimming training is a lake or the ocean, only swim when there is someone there who can rescue you if the need arises.

# taekwondo and weight training

I N THE 1960s, when taekwondo began to take hold in the Western world, weight training was not a part of everyday life. Gyms with an endless supply of free weights and weight training machines were not in every city. Serious weight training was most commonly left to those who wanted an enhanced physique.

In taekwondo's early days, weight training was, in fact, looked down upon in most taekwondo schools. It was believed that pumped-up muscles would slow down a practitioner's performance and reaction time.

With the advent of a deeper understanding of body mechanics, this misconception began to change, however. Taekwondo practitioners began to integrate weight training into their overall workout program.

## Understanding Taekwondo Weight Training

The physical training that taekwondo embraces is, by itself, an effective form of muscle-enhancing exercise. The muscles of your body naturally develop when you are putting them through the paces in your daily workouts. Still, focused weight training can be an important addition, which will help you in all aspects of your taekwondo training.

*Weight training can enhance your overall performance in taekwondo and help you to remain injury-free.*

Weight training, in relation to taekwondo, does not mean that you must develop your body to the level of a bodybuilding champion's. Instead, as a taekwondo practitioner, you will want to train with weights as part of a training program that will enhance your overall performance in the art and help you to remain free from injury.

## Weightlifting and Your Legs

For the average person who goes to a gym to lift weights, the legs are one of the primary focal points. The average person is not a taekwondo practitioner, however. As such, he or she does not encounter the advanced methods of leg development that are commonly part of taekwondo training.

Taekwondo training, in and of itself, is an unparalleled method of exercising your legs. As you are kicking virtually every day, your leg muscles are put through an intense training regimen that most weightlifters never experience. If you add an endurance training program to your overall tae-

Since a large portion of your taekwondo training involves leg, or kicking, exercises, which naturally enhance your leg muscles, your supplemental weight training should focus on your upper body.

kwondo workout—such as running, bicycling, or swimming—you will be providing your leg muscles with an additional form of muscle development.

For these reasons, it is not necessary to add weight training to further develop your legs. Therefore, taekwondo-oriented weight training is focused predominantly on the upper body. Enhanced arm, shoulder, back, and stomach muscles will all help you on your path to taekwondo mastery.

## Understanding Weightlifting

It is a common misconception that how much weight an individual can lift indicates his overall level of fitness. This is not true. In fact, lifting heavy weights is not the style of training a taekwondo practitioner should undergo.

The simple equation to weightlifting is that heavy weights equal body mass, while lighter weights tone and strengthen the body. The taekwondo practitioner, therefore, focuses his or her training on lifting lighter weights, in order to gain body definition and strength.

## Taekwondo Schools and Weightlifting

Some schools of taekwondo have elaborate weight training machines in the studio. Although these machines can be a great addition to your taekwondo experience, you can add weightlifting to your overall training program without them.

Virtually all schools of taekwondo have what are known as free weights. Free weights are gauged by specific poundage, or are designed to allow you to easily add or remove units to make them heavier or lighter. Free weights are an ideal tool for the taekwondo practitioner.

Taekwondo practitioners ideally use what are known as dumbbells for their weight training. Dumbbells are the type of weights that are held separately, one in each hand—as opposed to the longer bar, known as a barbell, which must be held with two hands.

The reason a taekwondo practitioner ideally uses dumbbells is that they isolate each weightlifting movement to a specific muscle group in the body. Using the larger barbell causes both sides of the body to lift the weight. What commonly occurs from this style of weight training is that the dominant side of the body lifts the majority of the weight and so becomes stronger. With dumbbells, movement is exactly targeted to a specific muscle group.

## Beginning to Lift

When you begin to lift weights, there are two terms you will need to become familiar with: "sets" and "reps." Sets are made up of a specific number of reps. Reps are the number of repetitions you perform in each weightlifting exercise. For example, you may lift a weight in a specific manner for ten reps. This will make up one set. The normal pattern for a beginning weightlifter is to do seven to twelve reps for each exercise and perform these lifts for a total of three sets.

Practice conscious weight training: breathe in before you lift and breathe out as you lift.

It is not a good idea to begin weight training by lifting the heaviest weight you can possibly elevate from the ground. This style of lifting is very damaging to the body. An ideal weight for a male taekwondo practitioner to begin with is twenty pounds. A female can begin with five pounds.

Furthermore, as you progress with your weight training experience, you do not need to continually increase the amount of weight you lift, as your body becomes stronger. You simply want your body to increase its strength, while remaining agile. Therefore, some taekwondo practitioners never increase the amount of weight they lift, but instead increase the number of sets they perform.

## Breath and Weight Training

There is an important method of breath control used in association with weight training. This technique teaches you to breathe in prior to lifting, and to breathe out as you lift the weight. This essential part of conscious weight training will help to keep you from straining your muscles.

When you breathe in, your muscles contract. When you breathe out, they relax. If your muscles are contracted as you lift a heavy weight, you can easily damage them. These lifting injuries occur most commonly in your stomach and groin region.

For this reason, it is essential to train yourself to automatically breathe out as you lift. Do not breathe in until your lift has been completed.

## Preparing to Train with Weights

As with all forms of physical exercise, you will need to stretch and warm up prior to weight training. The warmup for weight training can be as simple as performing a few forward bends, as you touch your toes. You can then rotate your body at the base of your spine, with your hands placed on your hips. Finally, you will want to shake loose your hands and arms, causing additional blood flow to be directed to these regions of your body.

To finish your warmup, you can perform ten jumping jacks. At this point, your body will be invigorated and you will be ready for weight training.

## The Primary Taekwondo Lifts

There are three primary weightlifting exercises the taekwondo practitioner should undertake: the curl, the frontal lift, and the bench press. Each of these exercises should be performed with a dumbbell, isolating each side of the body.

### The Curl

The curl is a simple lifting exercise designed to develop your biceps. To perform this exercise, sit down with your appropriately weighted dumbbell at your feet. Your lifting arm should be extended in a straight line toward the ground. Grasp the dumbbell, placing your elbow against your inner leg as a support. Then lift the dumbbell upward, toward your shoulder, as you bend your elbow (see Figure 15-1). You will feel your biceps being exercised.

Figure 15-1: The curl

The ideal way to perform this exercise is with one dumbbell. As you complete each set, switch sides and lift with your other arm. At first, you will want to perform this exercise for ten reps and three sets. As you progress, you can increase the weight of your dumbbell, and perform the number of reps and sets you feel is appropriate.

### The Forward Lift

To perform the forward lift, you take your appropriately weighted dumbbell and stand up. Your legs should be separated to support your body. Your back must be held erect.

When you are ready, lift the dumbbell up, directly in front of your body. Your lift will begin at the point where your arm is naturally extended, and will end when your arm and the dumbbell are parallel to the ground (see Figure 15-2).

As you lift, you will want to allow your elbow to be slightly bent. This will prevent your elbow joint from being injured.

The forward lift is an ideal exercise to perform to develop strength in your shoulder and back. It should initially be performed for ten reps and three sets. Remember, do not attempt to lift a weight that is too heavy, as this can damage your body.

Figure 15-2: Forward lift

### The Bench Press

The bench press can be performed either on a weight training bench or from the floor. The bench press is an ideal exercise to add strength to your triceps, chest, and back muscles.

Figure 15-3: Bench press

To perform this exercise, sit down, with an appropriately weighted dumbbell in each hand. When you feel you are ready, lie down onto your back. As you do so, bring the dumbbells up above your chest. When you are set, press the dumbbells upward, simultaneously, until your arms are almost fully extended (see Figure 15-3).

It is important in this exercise not to fully extend your arms and lock your elbows. Locking your elbows while you are supporting the weights can cause damage to the joints, so finish your lift just before your elbows are fully extended.

Once your lift has reached its pinnacle, lower your weights back to chest level. When you are ready, lift them again.

The bench press should be performed for ten reps and three sets at the beginning of your training. Increase the weight and the number of sets when you feel it is appropriate.

## Sit-ups

Although sit-ups are not an actual weightlifting exercise, they go hand in hand with taekwondo bodily development. Some teachers run their students through a prescribed number of sit-ups at every class. Others do not.

There are two distinct methods of performing sit-ups as part of taekwondo training. The traditional method dictates that you lie on your back with your knees bent and your feet flat on the floor, interlock your fingers behind your head, and then bend your body upward, for a prescribed number of times, touching your elbows to your knees.

Although this is the traditional method

Sit-ups are an essential element to your taekwondo training because, sooner or later, during training or sparring, you will be kicked in the stomach. If you have strengthened your stomach muscles by doing sit-ups, you will avoid internal injury.

**T**here are certain weightlifting machines that are designed to allow you to add weights to your sit-up training. Although these machines add the element of formal weight training to your sit-up experience, they are not a necessity.

of doing sit-ups, it has been linked to long-term lower back damage in some individuals. For this reason, a safer, equally effective method has been developed.

The second method of performing sit-ups is to lie on your back and place your hands, palms down, under your buttocks. When it is time to perform the exercise, you simultaneously lift your legs and back a few inches off the ground, and attempt to stay in this position. Try to develop the ability to hold this pose for one minute. Initially, this exercise can be practiced for five repetitions. As you progress in your bodily development, the number of times this exercise is performed can be increased to suit your training needs.

Although this method is not as dramatic or as cardioaerobically invigorating as the traditional sit-up, you may be surprised just how difficult it is to remain locked in this position for more than a few seconds. This is also an ideal way to develop your stomach muscles.

### Weight Training Precautions

Weight training has the potential to cause you to tear muscles and injure joints. This does not simply happen to the novice weight trainer or the individual who executes a lift in a sloppy manner—it can happen to anyone for any number of unforeseen reasons. To avoid injury, you must be very prudent in your weight training methods.

# taekwondo
# and ki

W HEN ONE THINKS about the systems of martial arts that embrace the understanding of ki, "internal energy," taekwondo is not one of the styles that commonly comes to mind. The Korean martial art of hapkido and the Japanese martial art of aikido are generally the styles one thinks of in relation to this ancient science. Although taekwondo is not commonly associated with the usage of ki, it is, nonetheless, a ki-oriented system of self-defense.

Taekwondo's usage of ki is not a metaphysical science that may be mastered only by ancient monks. Instead, ki is understood to be a method of consciously breathing, bringing amounts of life-giving oxygen into the body, and then expelling it when a technique is unleashed, in the form of a kihap, "a martial arts yell."

> In South Korea, the birthplace of taekwondo—and all over Asia, for that matter—ki is one of the first elements introduced to the new student of taekwondo.

## Breathing and Ki

It is understood that ki enters your body through your breath. If you breathe in a natural pattern, taking in full and deep breaths, then ki will naturally enter your body in large amounts. If, on the other hand, you breathe in shallow patterns and perform activities that are detrimental to your respiratory system, such as smoking, then ki will be inhibited from entering your body. As a result, your energy level will be low, and you will be easily fatigued while training.

One of the easiest methods of bringing extra amounts of ki into your body is to get into the habit of stopping what you are doing and taking several deep breaths at varying periods throughout the day. This is especially useful just prior to taekwondo training, as it will naturally invigorate your body and your mind.

## Tanjun

More than simply a science of breath control, the science of ki teaches the taekwondo practitioner how to find the body's center of gravity. This location is known in Korean as *tanjun*. This is understood to be the storehouse for ki.

Once this bodily location is identified, all of one's physical techniques are unleashed with a consciousness of this location. As a result, one remains balanced while performing all of the various movements associated with taekwondo.

Tanjun is a location approximately four inches below your navel. From this central location, tanjun extends two inches in width by two inches in height.

From the knowledge of your tanjun, you receive two benefits. First, your ability to isolate and use the movements of your body will be enhanced to a much higher degree, far surpassing that of the person who has no knowledge of his or her tanjun. Second, you will be able to readily and effectively channel ki throughout your entire body.

Figure 16-1a: Tanjun-defining exercise, Part 1

Figure 16-1b: Tanjun-defining exercise, Part 2

# Tanjun-Defining Exercise

Stand with your legs separated, approximately even with your shoulders. Your feet should be pointing forward. Allow your hands and fingers to be naturally extended at your side. Do not tighten the muscles of your body. Instead, remain semirelaxed.

Close your eyes and get comfortable in this standing posture for a few moments, as you begin to pay attention to the natural process of breath entering and exiting your body. When you feel you are ready, bring your hands to the front of your body as you pivot your wrists, until your open palms face upward, parallel to the ground (see Figure 16-1a). Allow your fingers to point toward one another. The next time you take a breath, breathe in deeply through your nose. As you do so, witness this breath travelling through your body, culminating in your tanjun.

As you perform this "in" breath, bring your hands slowly up your body until they reach your chest level (see Figure 16-1b). Once you have taken in a full breath, hold it in for a moment. Then, as you release it through your nose, pivot your palms over to a downward-facing position (see Figure 16-1c), and allow the breath to naturally leave your body, as your hands travel downward to their beginning positioning (see Figure 16-1d). As your breath leaves your body, witness this exhalation beginning from your tanjun. From this exercise,

Figure 16-1c: Tanjun-defining exercise, Part 3

Figure 16-1d: Tanjun-defining exercise, Part 4

the exact location of your body's center of gravity will clearly come into focus.

You should perform this tanjun breathing technique at least ten times a day, until you have clearly defined this bodily location. It may then be performed just prior to training or sparring, to refocus your ki energy.

## Understanding the Tanjun

The reason the tanjun is so revered, by true martial artists, is that it is understood to be the defining factor of physical balance. Once you have developed a clear knowledge of the location of your tanjun, you can begin to expand

The science of ki involves consciously breathing and finding your body's center of gravity, the *tanjun*.

upon this understanding and integrate it into all of your taekwondo technique. For example, while training in taekwondo, when you move your body from one location to the next, begin to take notice of how your center of gravity is reacting to your movement. When you are practicing kicking, begin to observe how each movement you make feels in relation to your center of gravity. When you felt off balance, or you lost your balance, how conscious were you of your tanjun? By making a conscious effort to concentrate on your tanjun as you perform the various taekwondo techniques, you will achieve a refined level of balance in all of your physical movements.

## The Kihap

Advanced practitioners of taekwondo give little thought to the fact that they breathe in, direct the breath to their tanjun, and then release it with a kihap, during every technique. Because they have consciously developed this ability, it has become subconscious.

The novice taekwondo practitioner, however, also does not think when he performs a technique. This is why most novice students prefer not to kihap when they perform the various techniques. They do not understand the meaning of the action and, thus, are not truly utilizing this advanced science of self-defense.

As has been described, ki enters your body via your breath. The advanced practitioner directs this breath to his or her tanjun, where it is released when an offensive or defensive technique is performed. For the novice student to truly tap into this source of internal energy, he or she must take the time to develop the ability to truly utilize ki. That can only be done through practice.

To begin your ki training, just prior to performing a technique, consciously breathe in, while directing the breath to your tanjun. As you unleash the technique, rapidly breathe out from your tanjun, in the form of a kihap.

No one can force you to perform taekwondo in this fashion, but if you wish to truly tap into the power of ki, this must be your first step. In time, it will become a natural process, and you will be able to utilize ki without a thought.

# part 5
# training drills

**T**HE TRAINING you receive in the taekwondo class will guide you down the road to new physical mastery and a sense of self-confidence. However, training in the taekwondo class is only your first step to taekwondo mastery. As a taekwondo practitioner, you must take what you learn in class and move this knowledge onto the level of true personal understanding. There is only one way to achieve this result—that is, by integrating a program of personal exploration into your overall training regimen.

# chapter 17
# kicking drills

**O**NE OF THE KEY ELEMENTS to advancing in taekwondo is kicking drills. Kicking drills are divided into two categories. The first is for refining your kicks—making them as perfect as possible. As it is essential to deliver your kicks in a precise manner, whenever you encounter an opponent, this level of training is designed to train and retrain you in delivering specific kicks in the most exact manner possible.

The second level of taekwondo kicking-drill training is designed to teach you how to deploy your kicks in both a focused and continuous manner. Because you can never be sure that a single technique will be enough to overcome your opponent, you must learn how to deliver exactly targeted kicks, and then go on to the next and the next, in the most rapid and precise manner possible, until your opponent is defeated.

Each of the following kicking drills will help you to refine your kicking techniques and come to a deeper understanding of taekwondo's kicking arsenal, in relation to your own body mechanics. As the advanced taekwondo practitioner understands, one's participation in taekwondo is an ongoing evolution that never ends. These kicking drills are designed to aid you in your continued growth as a practitioner.

## Refining Your Kicks

There is no greater tool in the taekwondo practitioner's training arsenal than that of repetition. No matter how many times you have performed a technique, by performing it again, you will come to a new and deeper understanding of the mechanics that make up each individual technique. Through ongoing practice, you will come to understand new applications for even the most basic kicks. It is for this reason that all advanced masters of the art continually train in the basic elements of taekwondo.

There are six styles of kicking drills that are used to develop and refine a tae-kwondo practitioner's kicking expertise:

1. The slow-speed kicking drill
2. The medium-speed kicking drill
3. The rapid-speed kicking drill
4. The interval kicking drill
5. The dynamic tension kicking drill
6. The underwater kicking drill

## The Slow-Speed Kicking Drill

The slow-speed kicking drill is an ideal way to begin each of your taekwondo training sessions. It teaches you, the taekwondo practitioner, how to truly master the basic kicks of the art.

For the slow-speed kicking drill, you enter into a fighting stance and perform each of the basic kicks in the slowest manner possible. You begin with the front kick, move on to the side kick, and finish up with the roundhouse kick. Perform each of these kicking techniques a minimum of ten times per side, to develop and train both of your legs equally.

The slow-speed kicking drill is an ideal way for you to truly master a kick—this is one of the best training methods you can commit to performing on a daily basis.

The slow-speed kicking drill is not limited to taekwondo's basic kicks. It is an ideal method for developing a precise understanding of the more advanced kicks, as well. Simply begin with the three basic kicks and then move forward to the more advanced kicking technique you wish to refine.

As all of the advanced kicking techniques of taekwondo are based on these three primary kicks, until you have completely mastered each one of them, you will not be able to perform the more advanced techniques with any level of expertise.

## The Medium-Speed Kicking Drill

Unlike the slow-speed kicking drill, the medium-speed kicking drill cannot be performed as the only exercise drill of the session. You should only use this training method after doing the slow-speed kicking drill, because it is designed to take you to the next level of understanding in the dynamics of the taekwondo kick.

To practice the medium-speed kicking drill, begin immediately after you have performed at least ten repetitions of each of the three basic kicks, on each leg, with the slow-speed kicking drill. To begin, enter into a fighting stance and perform each of the three basic kicks: the front kick, the side kick, and the roundhouse kick. This time, increase the speed just a bit, to about half the speed of a kick done with full power.

By training in this manner, you will begin to understand the dynamics of each kick, as it is traveling at a faster rate of speed. From this, you will learn how to master the kick, developing your ability to deliver it properly when it is traveling toward its target.

## The Rapid-Speed Kicking Drill

The rapid-speed kicking drill serves two purposes. First of all, it is a great form of aerobic exercise that strengthens your leg muscles. Second, it teaches you how to rapidly deliver kicks in the most precise manner possible.

As with the medium-speed kicking drill, this drill serves no purpose unless you have begun with the slow-speed kicking drill and then gone on to the medium-speed kicking drill. The entire purpose of these kicking drills is to train you to truly understand the body mechanics of taekwondo kicks when they are unleashed at varying rates of speed. Although it is tempting to show off your kicking prowess by kicking as high and as fast as possible, that is not the point of these exercises. You must perform them in an evolving order.

When performing the rapid-speed kicking drill, you will again focus upon the three primary kicks of taekwondo: the front kick, the side kick, and the roundhouse kick. Enter into a fighting stance and perform ten kicks with each leg. Kick as rapidly as possible, at a precise imaginary target. From this training, you will gain a new understanding of the effect each kick has on your body as it is rapidly unleashed.

## The Interval Kicking Drill

The interval kicking drill should be performed after you have progressed through the slow-speed kicking drill, the medium-speed kicking drill, and the rapid-speed kicking drill. To perform this drill, you will again focus on taekwondo's primary kicks and perform them ten or more times, per leg.

To begin this drill, enter into a fighting stance and very slowly unleash a front kick. Then immediately deliver a rapid front kick. Then immediately follow up by performing a front kick at medium speed. Continue this interval training process until you have performed ten or more front kicks, then switch legs and begin the process again.

This kicking drill is an exercise in body-mind coordination. In addition, it allows you to immediately experience how each of taekwondo's basic kicks feels, when unleashed at a different rate of speed and with a different intensity. This is an ideal drill to culminate with, in order to train your body for the different types of kicks that must be unleashed in a sparring competition.

## The Dynamic Tension Kicking Drill

Whereas the medium-speed kicking drill, the rapid-speed kicking drill, and the interval kicking drill all build on the slow-speed kicking drill, this is not the case with the dynamic tension kicking drill. You can certainly follow up those exercises with this drill, but it is not required that you do so. This kicking drill can be performed on its own. What you will do is, again, return to taekwondo's three basic kicks and unleash them with the muscles of your legs tightened.

To begin, enter into a fighting stance. When you feel you are ready, perform a front kick, very slowly, with the muscles of your striking leg held very tight. Bring the kick up to its target point, and then slowly bring it back to its stationary position.

The term "dynamic tension" refers to the technique of tightening the muscles of a specific region of the body.

The purpose of the dynamic tension kicking drill is threefold: (1) it is designed to give you a deeper understanding of how each kick is delivered, (2) it teaches you which muscles are used to deliver each of taekwondo's basic kicks, and (3) it helps to develop your leg muscles.

## The Underwater Kicking Drill

If you have access to a swimming pool, it can be the ideal place for your ongoing training in executing the perfect taekwondo kick. The reason kicking underwater is such an effective training method is that the liquid environment holds your body suspended. When you deliver a kicking technique underwater, you can watch it, from its inception to its end point, as if it were presented in slow motion. From this, you will be able to judge its form, structure, and implementation.

To begin the underwater kicking drill, enter a pool and take up a fighting stance, at a point where the water is approximately chest deep. When you feel ready, deliver a front kick. Do not attempt to deliver it as quickly as possible; simply allow it to slowly and precisely travel to its natural end point. Throughout the execution of this kick, witness how you feel, how your body is reacting, and how the kick is making progress. When you have completed the technique, allow your leg to remain locked in its end position for a moment. Study your structure and your form.

Once you have completed the first application of this training drill, return to your start position and perform the kick for a second time. This time, try to unleash the kick in a more precise manner than you did in your first attempt. At the conclusion of the kick, again study your structure and form.

Perform this exercise up to ten times per kick, per side. Each time you do so, attempt to make your kick's execution more precise and exact.

This kicking drill can be used with all of taekwondo's kicks. From it, you will be able to develop and redevelop your kicking arsenal, raising your techniques to a new level of expertise.

# chapter 18
# target training

**T**ARGET TRAINING is an essential element for your continuing evolution as a taekwondo practitioner. By focusing on an object and then striking it, you come to understand the dynamics of combat. You are allowed to experience what it actually feels like to aim at a specific target and then unleash an offensive technique at it.

*The most common method of target training in taekwondo is to target a hanging bag.*

## The Hanging Bag

Hanging bags are designed to help taekwondo students develop their kicking focus and their kicking power. The hanging bags are such an essential element to taekwondo training that you will find one suspended in virtually every taekwondo studio in the world.

The hanging bag is approximately four feet long, and comes in two primary weights. There is the heavy bag, which weighs approximately 100 pounds, and the medium bag, which weighs approximately fifty pounds.

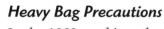

### Heavy Bag Precautions

In the 1960s and into the 1970s, when taekwondo was taking hold in the West, there were only a couple of companies that made hanging bags. At that time, hanging bags were primarily designed to be used by boxers, who wanted them to be as heavy and firm as possible. This gave the boxer the sensation of punching a human body.

Although this design was ideally suited to boxers, it was not an ideal design

> Undoubtedly, as each of us is either dominant on our right or left side, one side of your body will be more powerful. Practice alternate leg kicking drills to develop both sides of your body into one cohesive unit.

for the taekwondo practitioner. These heavy bags caused a lot of unnecessary injuries, because striking them with a powerful kicking technique is much different from punching them. The muscles of the legs are not only much larger than those of the arms, they are also much stronger. Therefore, when taekwondo practitioners repeatedly kicked a heavy bag, the impact was much more powerful than could be unleashed by the hands. Although this sounds like a good thing, it was not so good for the body of the taekwondo practitioner.

From kicking the heavy bag, many taekwondo practitioners of that era incurred joint injuries. Therefore, the heavy bag should only be used for a very specific style of controlled training by the advanced practitioner of taekwondo. Today, the heavy bag is most commonly used by the experienced practitioner who wishes to develop the ability to launch very powerful stepping and jumping kicks.

## The Medium Bag

The medium bag is an ideal tool for practicing and refining taekwondo kicking techniques. As the medium bag is much lighter and less dense than the heavy bag, the sensation of striking against it closely resembles that of unleashing a kick into the body of a person. By training with the medium bag, you come to understand what it feels like to actually make contact with an opponent.

### Medium Bag Training Exercise One

Virtually all of taekwondo's kicking and punching arsenal can be practiced on the medium bag. A good method of training is to start out with one specific kick, such as the roundhouse.

Begin slowly and kick the bag lightly several times as you begin your bag training. By kicking slowly at first, you will learn how the kick is most properly unleashed against your target, and how it feels when your foot makes impact.

As you progress with this exercise, begin to kick the bag with more speed and more power. With each increase, you will learn how it feels to make impact with the kick at that specific speed and that specific power.

Finish the exercise by delivering several very fast and very powerful round-house kicks to the bag. Not only will this provide you with a bit of endurance training, but it will also give you a sense of how it feels in the midst of combat when you must deliver one rapid technique after the next.

It is essential that after you finish training one side of your body, you immediately switch sides and train the other. Although everyone favors one side of his or her body, you cannot allow this to dominate your taekwondo training. You must become as proficient with both sides of your body as possible.

## Medium Bag Training Exercise Two

Your next level of training with the medium bag begins by using the same kick that you used before—the roundhouse. This time, instead of performing kicking techniques delivered from only one side, you will employ both of your legs.

Again, face off with the bag and begin slowly. Deliver a slow set of ten roundhouse kicks to the bag. As you do, alternate your legs with each kick. For example, begin with your right leg, then use your left, then back to your right. With this style of training, you will experience how it feels to unleash multiple attacks from each side of your body.

> While the heavy bag is used by advanced students to improve their ability to launch powerful stepping and jumping kicks, the medium bag is an ideal tool to use to develop and focus your overall kicking skill.

When you have finished your tenth kick, halt the exercise and rest for a moment. Make a conscious mental note of how you felt when performing your kicking techniques in this manner.

After you have rested for a few moments, turn up the speed and power on this exercise, and kick at a medium rate. With each kick, again, feel how the evolving speed affects your body, and note the impact that your increased power has on the bag. After the tenth kick, halt the exercise and rest.

In the final phase of this exercise, kick the bag with full speed and power. As you do so, be careful to study the location of the bag before you unleash your kick. With added power, there will be added movement. This will teach you targeting insight and will help you when you actually enter into competition.

This is just one example of how the medium bag may be used as a targeting and skill-developing tool in taekwondo. The roundhouse kick is not the only kick that can be applied to this exercise. Practice with a few different techniques and see how each of them works for you.

As you progress with this exercise, over a period of weeks and months, begin to notice how your kicking techniques have evolved—how did they feel different this time, from the last time? This will provide you with a window into your ongoing development in taekwondo.

### Mistakes with the Medium Bag

The common mistake many budding taekwondo students make when they first encounter the medium bag is to see how hard they can make it swing when they kick it. It seems such a great accomplishment to send one of these bags powerfully swinging on its chain. This is fun, but it has little to do with your ongoing development as a martial artist. Your kicks will naturally become more powerful as you continue to train in taekwondo. Therefore, you do not need to show off to prove this point.

# The Striking Ball

The small striking ball is another striking target that is ideally suited to taekwondo training; it can increase your focus and improve your timing for both punching and kicking techniques. Many companies market these striking balls, which range in size from the size of a basketball down to the size of a tennis ball. Each comes with an appropriately sized elastic rope, which allows you to suspend it between the ceiling and the floor.

The striking ball is an ideal training target, because when you strike at one, you instantly know if you have hit it correctly. If you have, the ball moves in a linear pattern, back and forth. If you have not, the ball spins awkwardly out of control.

## Striking Ball Placement

Whenever you position one of these striking balls, always locate it in the position you would actually strike on your opponent's body—for example, the head, the solar plexus, or the groin region. By locating the target in an appropriate strike zone, you will learn which offensive techniques are most effective for that region of your opponent's body, and which strikes can be most powerfully delivered.

In many ways, the suspended striking ball is an ideal training target. Its size makes it very difficult to strike correctly. Therefore, it accurately focuses your attacks. This type of training allows you to develop acute focus and proper striking technique.

## Striking Ball Training Exercise One

The striking balls are obviously much easier to hit with your hands than with your feet. Therefore, begin this exercise by straight-punching at your target.

With each impact your fist makes, notice how the ball reacts. Watch it move away from you, and then strike it when it has sprung back toward you. To begin to integrate timing training into this exercise, let the ball pass you every few times, as you lean out of its path of travel. This will help you learn how to quickly move out of the path of an oncoming attack.

After a few minutes of experiencing how the ball reacts to your hand strikes, unleash a front kick as the ball is returning in your direction. Immediately, you will notice that your front kick does not have the same linear impact that your hand strikes did. This

> The reason it is essential to develop both of your legs to their highest possible potential is that in competition you must be able to deliver one kick after another, until you ultimately defeat your opponent. Taekwondo kicking drills have been developed to help you achieve this result.

is your next level of taekwondo development—learning to kick the striking ball with a front kick that will cause it to recoil in a completely linear pattern.

The reason your front kick should cause this style of impact is that you want its power to be driven directly in front of you and straight into your target. Many budding taekwondo practitioners believe that the higher their kick is, the better it is. This is not true. In fact, a high kick usually reveals how little overall power your kicking technique has. Therefore, height is not your ultimate goal. Your goal is focused and directed power.

As you begin this training exercise for the second time, start by striking the ball with a straight punching technique. As you integrate a front kick into your program, attempt to cause the ball to travel directly forward. This will obviously take some practice. Do not be discouraged if you cannot achieve this motion in your early attempts at this training exercise. Simply continue to practice, and your ability to deliver a front kick in a precisely linear fashion will be developed. This is the purpose of taekwondo training drills—

to make you a better martial artist, with techniques as precisely delivered as possible.

## Striking Ball Training Exercise Two

As you now understand, the striking ball is a great tool to help you to develop proper focus and execution in your punching and kicking techniques. This next exercise will help you hone your skills for many of taekwondo's kicks.

To begin this exercise, take your position in front of the striking ball as you enter into a fighting stance. Now, as quickly as you can, without thinking or spending more than a moment focusing, throw a roundhouse kick toward your target. What will probably happen is that you will miss the ball, or strike it indirectly.

What you initially learn from this exercise is that your targeting is not exact. This is especially true when you are forced to throw a technique in less than ideal circumstances. For this reason, you must begin to narrowly focus your kicks.

Enter into a fighting stance and face off against the striking ball for the second time. This time, focus on the ball and slowly execute your roundhouse kick. Do not attempt to kick the ball as hard as you can. Simply plan to make very light contact with it.

This time, no doubt, you will make a precise strike against your target. This teaches you that when your techniques are controlled, they can be exact. The problem is, however, that in competition and on the street, you do not have the time or the opportunity to truly focus your offensive techniques. Therefore, you must develop this ability while training.

For the next step of this kicking drill, you slowly kick at the striking ball, with your roundhouse kick, ten times. This allows you to develop your focus.

As soon as you have completed your tenth kick, immediately deliver five very fast roundhouse kicks to the bag. What will no doubt occur is that your kicks will not be as exactly focused as the slow ones were.

What you will learn from this segment of the training drill is that, even though you were focused with the slow kicking, everything changed the moment your speed and intensity increased. Therefore, you must be constantly willing to redevelop your skill of focusing, as each combative situation changes.

This training exercise is an ideal drill to test your focus and coordination with the various taekwondo kicks. By frequently returning to this drill, you will be able to monitor your progress in focus and kicking application for all of taekwondo's kicks.

Taekwondo training is an ongoing process. Training drills teach you how to refine your techniques to make them useful in all situations. From this drill and others, you will be able to define your weak points and learn to overcome them. For this reason, never be discouraged if you do not perform a technique with absolute accuracy, as the walk down the path of taekwondo is an ongoing, never ending learning experience.

# Multiple-Leg Kicking Drills

In each taekwondo class, you are taught various applications of multiple kicks. You will be told to deliver a front kick, followed by a side kick, ending up with a back kick, and so on. Although this is a fine method to learn the basics of kicking combinations, it is you who must take this understanding to the next level and make multiple kicking work for you. The following are a couple of drills that can aid you in the process.

## The Front-Kick, Side-to-Side Kicking Drill

To begin this kicking drill, enter into a fighting stance. When you feel it is time to begin, rapidly switch your front leg to a rear position. Accomplish this change of legs by performing a very low jump off the ground, as your legs change positions.

The moment your feet have touched the ground, launch a front kick from your rear leg. Upon completion of the kick, immediately place your striking leg down directly in front of you. The second it hits the ground, again perform the change-of-legs jump and bring it back to the rear. Again, launch a front kick with this rear leg.

Continue this training drill for ten to twenty kicks. The moment you have completed your final kick, quickly switch legs and go through the drill again with the opposite leg.

This training drill teaches you to rapidly deliver front kicks, with each of your legs, to one central location. Not only is it a great form of imaginary target training, but it also provides an excellent cardioaerobic workout.

## The Back-Kick Training Drill

The back kick is a very effective offensive and defensive weapon. This has been proven in an untold number of taekwondo tournaments. Although the back kick is a great weapon, it is rarely used in an offensive fashion—mainly because few people know how to unleash this kick correctly and effectively.

To begin this exercise, enter into a fighting stance. Glance over your shoulder, as if you had an opponent behind you, and find a point where you can focus your attention and your attack. The second you have located this point—your own image in a mirror, for example, or a point on the wall some distance off—launch your first back kick. The moment you have completed its execution, immediately launch a second one from the opposite leg. Follow through with this technique and regain your footing in a forward stance.

Now that you have regained your footing, ask yourself these questions, "Did I stay on target?" "Did I lose sight of my target?" "Did I move forward in a straight line?" "Did I come to rest in a ready position, or was I off balance?" These are all telling questions as to your overall execution of the multiple back kick.

Once you have answered these questions, reposition yourself and release two rapid back-kicking techniques. Once you have completed these kicks, again check your position and decide if these kicks were delivered correctly and effectively.

Once you have mastered the two back-kick techniques, raise the number of back kicks to be performed up to five. As you perform each one, maintain balance, and drive powerfully forward into your target. At the conclusion of the five back kicks, again study your body position and decide if you performed the kicks in an appropriate manner.

The reason the back kick is such an effective offensive weapon, particularly in competition, is that you are only exposing your back to your opponent. Thus, opponents have little counterstrike area to target.

This training tool is so effective because it forces your body to learn to coordinate and move in a completely unnatural pattern—backward. From this, you will gain new mastery of bodily coordination and kicking technique.

# chapter 19
# partner training

ARTNER TRAINING is an ideal way to develop your taekwondo offensive and defensive skills. By working out with another individual, you learn that human movement is predictable. Extensive practice and observation of this kind teaches you to recognize the physical movements that precede and then follow the various styles of punches and kicks.

## Focus-Glove Training

A focus glove is a small padded training tool that is held in the hand of your training partner. There are many varieties of focus gloves on the market today, but they all serve a similar purpose: developing your hand, foot, and eye coordination, and making you a more skillful practitioner of taekwondo. Commonly, when you train with focus gloves, your training partner holds a glove in one or both hands as you direct various offensive and defensive techniques toward it.

Training with focus gloves will help you to develop your hand, foot, and eye coordination.

### Single-Glove Training Drill

At the outset of your training with a focus glove, you will want to develop your focus, your directed power, and your understanding of multiple-kicking techniques. An ideal way to achieve this is to have your training partner hold a single focus glove and remain in a stationary position. You will begin in a fighting stance, and your training partner will call out techniques to you: "front kick," "side kick," "roundhouse kick." As he or she calls out these techniques, you will kick the glove with the appropriate technique.

From this initial exercise you will gain a basic understanding of how one tae-kwondo kick follows the last, how your body reacts to each kick, and how to best deliver each technique with an ever-growing understanding of focus. The formative value of this exercise makes it an essential training tool for every taekwondo practitioner.

## Coordination Training Drill

To develop your ability to strike precisely with a specific technique, an ideal training method is to have your partner hold one focus glove in each hand. You will begin this exercise by entering into a fighting stance. Your training partner will begin a few feet in front of you. When you both are ready, he or she will begin to call out techniques. For example, "Front kick, right foot." You will then deliver a front kick to your partner's focus glove with your right foot. "Roundhouse kick, left foot." You will then deliver a roundhouse kick with your left foot, and so on. While calling out these techniques, your partner will move randomly across the training floor. This will require that you first locate your target and then unleash the appropriate technique.

Of course, it would be easy for your training partner to move the glove out of the way, as your kick or punch was traveling toward its target, but that is not the purpose of this training drill. Your partner will move, but will keep the focus glove in place long enough for you to make striking contact with it. He or she will then move on to calling out the next technique or set of techniques.

It is a good idea to continually return to this drill, because it trains your body and mind to quickly react to whatever technique is called out, and then to find an appropriate target. Delivering your own choice of technique against the focus gloves is also an effective method of training, but it is not nearly as difficult as being told which kick or punch to unleash.

## Timing and Accuracy Training Drill One

To begin the timing and accuracy training drill, face off with a training part-ner who is holding two focus gloves. When you are both ready, your training partner will signal you and then begin to move.

In the early stages of this drill, your training partner should move slowly. Speed is not your initial objective in this training exercise, but safety is.

Your partner will continue to move around the room. In the early stages, he or she will move while positioning a focus glove in an obvious strike location. For example, a glove turned downward toward the ground will signal you to deliver a front kick. A glove held at face level will tell you to deliver a straight punch.

Your partner and the focus gloves will continue to travel. This will help you to develop the ability to successfully move in and strike a target that is in motion. From this exercise, not only will you develop exact targeting skills, but you will learn which technique is most effective at which distance.

## Timing and Accuracy Training Drill Two

In the previous exercise, your training partner was moving, while positioning the focus gloves for you to strike. This stage of the exercise is much more demanding—not only on you, as the person unleashing the attacks, but also on your training partner, who is holding the gloves. This difficulty is due to the fact that the focus gloves will be in constant motion.

> Holding the training gloves for your partner can provide essential insight into technique—look at this as another opportunity to enhance your training.

In all physical conflicts, whether they take place in a formal sparring match or on the street, two people are in motion. This exercise in advanced taekwondo training teaches you to deal with this situation.

To begin this exercise, face off with your training partner. When you are both ready, your training partner will begin to move. This time, however, he or she will not allow the focus gloves to wait for your strike—instead, they will be in motion. If your training partner sees your technique coming, he or she will move the focus glove out of the way.

From this style of training, you will learn that your techniques must be rapid and exactly focused, if you want them to make striking contact. Therefore, you must develop the skills to deliver your strikes in the most precise manner possible.

A word of caution is necessary here: At this level of training, you are expected to have substantial control over your offensive technique. You should not throw out wild techniques that will strike your training partner if they miss the focus glove.

## Being a Training Partner

Although most people prefer to be the one aiming at the focus gloves, there is much to be learned from holding them, as well. Unleashing attacks toward your training partner is only one small part of gaining deeper insight into taekwondo. As you hold the focus gloves and watch your partner unleashing attacks directed toward them, you gain incredible insight into the essence of offensive attacks. Thus, holding the gloves is an essential element in your growing understanding of taekwondo.

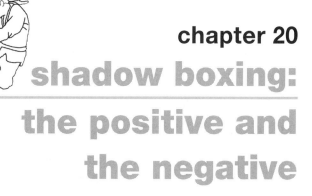

# shadow boxing: the positive and the negative

**A** COMMON FORM of taekwondo practice involves what has come to be known as "shadow boxing." Shadow boxing involves randomly punching or kicking at imaginary targets in the air. Although this can be an effective way of warming up and getting your cardiovascular system working, this form of practice can have several negative results—not the least of which is damage to your own body.

Punching and kicking at imaginary targets in the air is a fine method of loosening up your body prior to formal training. When used in a controlled manner, this style of training can be good exercise for your muscles.

Undirected punching and kicking should not give you the mistaken idea that you are actually developing focus with your techniques, however. Quite the contrary is true, in fact. As you are punching and kicking haphazardly into the air, you may believe you are directing your fists and feet where you want them to go, but you have no actual way of measuring the effectiveness of your attack. You have no way of knowing whether or not you actually made contact with the imaginary target you had in mind.

## Mirror Training

Powerfully punching or kicking toward a mirror is another method of shadow boxing that taekwondo students employ in hopes of honing their skills. You can develop more precisely styled hand- and foot-striking techniques by watching your punches and kicks in a mirror; however, again, you have no actual measure of whether or not you have made contact with your intended target.

Most taekwondo students certainly believe that they can direct their fist or foot toward an object and make striking contact with the target. In some cases, this may be true, especially if the target does not move. But how many times in a physical confrontation does your opponent remain stationary and allow you to effortlessly punch or kick at him? This is the major problem with relying upon shadow boxing as a primary training tool.

## Shadow Kicking

The shadow boxing style of training is also commonly used among taekwondo practitioners who have mastered the basic elements of some kicking applications. They will powerfully drive their kicks into the air, in an uncontrolled manner. Although this method of kick development is taught in many taekwondo schools, it is one of the most damaging things you can do to the joints of your knees, hips, and ankles.

When you powerfully launch a kick into the open air, you snap your leg up and out, generally as high as your current level of stretching will allow your leg to go. By practicing your kicking technique in this fashion, you do not develop any degree of focus, and you can easily damage your leg joints. For example, by propelling your leg into the air, while unleashing a front kick, you are forcefully snapping your knee. As time goes on, this type of powerful snapping to the knee will cause your cartilage and ligaments to stretch unnaturally and possibly tear. For some, it may take a long time for this to occur; for others, it may occur much sooner.

While shadow boxing is an effective way to warm up your body prior to a training session, it is not an effective means of target training.

Very similar practices are used with the various other kicks of taekwondo. The powerful air-driven side kick, for example, puts a great deal of pressure on the tendons in your hips. The powerful air-launched roundhouse kick can damage both your hip and knee joints. Therefore, attempting to powerfully launch kicks into the air is not a good method of solitary training.

# Effective Shadow Boxing

The two primary reasons for training in taekwondo are physical fitness and the ability to successfully defend yourself if you ever need to do so. Therefore, to accomplish both, you must refine your solo training methods so that you will not only gain superior technique and focusing ability but also maintain your health.

The obvious question is: "What type of effective training can I practice if I do not have a striking bag to develop my focus, and I have no training partner to hold focus gloves for me?" There are several very effective and safe ways for you to develop your taekwondo skills when you are training alone. The key in

The most important aspect of solo training is to remain in control of your technique.

solo training is that no technique—no punch, no kick—should be allowed to control your body. You must remain in control over it. That is, never let muscle-driven, forced momentum drive your punches or kicks through the open air. As you now understand, this can do damage to your body. Maintain control at all times. On this basis, we can begin to view some effective solo training methods.

## Open-Air Punching and Kicking

To begin, let's consider what type of open-air punching and kicking is safe and effective for focus development.

It is essential to keep in mind, especially in shadow boxing, that no punch or kick should be allowed to control the momentum of your body. Just as in the case of a punch or kick directed toward a human target, you want to maintain control over all of your bodily movements. This will allow you to refine your technique and keep your body free from injury.

Prior to beginning proper shadow boxing, you should loosen up your arms, shoulders, torso, neck, and legs by stretching. This is easily accomplished by rotating your shoulders, back and forward, and then shaking your arms loose and moving them around a bit. You then slowly rotate your neck around, and follow up by rotating your body at the base of your spine. You then shake your legs loose and perform a few easy stretches. With this, you will release any initial muscle tension and cause increased blood circulation throughout your body. You are ready to begin your practice.

## Focused Shadow Boxing

To begin, you will need to find a target to focus on. This does not have to be a target you will strike. It can be a location on the mirror or an object some distance in front of you. In either case, this object will give you an ideal to focus your attack upon. By punching and kicking at this object, instead of just wildly throwing your techniques into the open air, you will not only develop your punching and kicking focus, but you will be able to immediately tell if your punches or kicks would have made contact, if the target had been real.

In the beginning of this refined style of shadow boxing training, you will probably be amazed at how often the power of your arm or leg will throw your punch or kick off its intended target. As time goes on and you continue this training drill, however, you will learn how to deliver your punches and kicks in a way that compensates for the muscle strength of your arms and legs. Eventually, you will constantly seem to make contact with your imaginary target.

## Shadow Boxing and Movement

As time progresses, and you become more competent with your shadow-boxing targeting, you will want to add movement to your training. An ideal way to advance to this level of shadow-boxing training is to begin in a stationary position and deliver several punches and kicks toward your target. When you feel you are well focused, begin to move around as if you were sparring with an opponent. Then, again attempt to deliver focused hand techniques and kicks toward your target. Initially, no doubt, you will not make focused contact, because the change in pattern from stationary focus to movement has shifted your perspective—but keep trying. You will eventually find your focus and begin to make contact with your imaginary target.

Although shadow boxing can be a great addition to your taekwondo training, you must remember that you are targeting an imaginary object. Therefore, this should not be your only form of solo training. Bag and glove training truly add to your overall understanding of the art, and hone your ability to make real contact with a physical object.

# part 6
# free-sparring
# and competition

**F**REE-SPARRING IS the single most important element in a taekwondo practitioner's study of the art. Through free-sparring,
the taekwondo student learns how to unleash offensive attacks
and defend against oncoming assaults. Without free-sparring, taekwondo
would just be a system of martial arts based solely on combative philosophy.

# sparring and competition

## Free-Sparring

There are three levels of free-sparring, or *kyorugi*, employed in taekwondo:

1. No contact
2. Semicontact
3. Full contact

### No-Contact Sparring

No-contact sparring is used in the taekwondo studio to train the novice student in the fundamentals of free-sparring. With this style of sparring, new students are allowed to guide their techniques in the direction of their sparring opponents, but no contact is to be made.

The reason for the no-contact rule is that beginning-level students do not possess the focus or control necessary to be sure of making only light contact with their techniques. Training in no-contact sparring allows them to begin to learn how it feels to spar with an opponent, while avoiding injury.

### Light-Contact Sparring

Light-contact sparring is the style of free-sparring that is commonly employed in the taekwondo studio by the intermediate and advanced students. Light-contact sparring allows them to unleash the various offensive techniques that make up their offensive arsenal, while making light contact with their opponent. Sparring in this manner keeps injuries to a minimum and allows the practitioner to experience the realities of hand-to-hand combat.

## Full-Contact Sparring

Full-contact sparring is used predominantly by advanced practitioners of taekwondo who are directing their training toward tournament-level competition. In full-contact sparring, martial artists are allowed to deliver the full power of their offensive techniques, to the appropriate strike points on the body of their opponents.

# Competitive Sparring

To begin to understand taekwondo's evolution as a competitive sport, it must be understood that there are two primary levels of competition that the taekwondo practitioner has the opportunity to compete in: (1) the open tournament and (2) the Olympic-style taekwondo competition.

As open tournaments were the first to expose taekwondo's kicking prowess to the world, we can begin by taking a look at the factors that make up these events.

## Taekwondo and the Open Tournament

The open tournament, commonly known as a "karate tournament," was the backbone of Western tournament fighting throughout the 1960s and 1970s, and into the 1980s. Although these events are still very much a part of modern martial arts culture, they have taken a backseat where taekwondo is concerned. This is largely because taekwondo has become an official Olympic sport, and much of the taekwondo practitioner's competitive focus is geared toward Olympic-style events.

The word *kyorugi* is the Korean term used to describe "free-sparring."

At the karate tournament, practitioners from all styles of martial arts congregate and compete against one another. The first event held at these tournaments is normally the forms competition. Here, practitioners from the various systems of martial arts demonstrate their expertise by performing both nonweapon and weapon-oriented forms. Many times, this portion of the event features elaborate and beautiful demonstrations of a practitioner's art.

Competitive sparring has been a mainstay of taekwondo since it was first established in Korea, and proved popular when it travelled to Western shores, where, by the early 1960s, "karate tournaments" were large events.

Following the forms competitions, the sparring segment of the tournament gets under way. This usually begins with the junior martial artists taking the floor. These young competitors range in age from five-year-olds to early teenagers. Once this segment of the tournament is complete, adult competition begins.

At the open tournament, the adult competitors are divided into weight and belt rankings, including the lower (yellow and orange) belt division, the mid-level (blue and green) belt division, and the advanced (red and brown) belt division. The lower ranks begin first, followed in turn by the advancing ranks. Finally, the black belts take to the floor, and the tournament culminates with the black-belt sparring competition.

At the open tournament, protective gear is virtually never required and is rarely worn. The practitioners simply wear their martial arts uniforms.

The fighting competition at these events takes place within a square area of generally twelve feet by twelve feet. These defining lines are commonly taped onto the floor of a rented gymnasium. Sparring is only allowed within these lines. If a participant steps out of the lines, the match is halted, the opponents are called back to the center of the ring, and the match is restarted.

Matches are normally scored by three judges. The center judge referees the match. He calls the competitors to the ring, has them bow to one another, and oversees the match. There are also two side judges who call points.

To distinguish the two competitors, for scoring purposes, one of them is commonly provided with a white cloth ribbon and the other with a red one, which they tie around their belts. The judges then hold up a red or white flag when a scoring point has been made.

The open tournaments are commonly scored on a three-point system, meaning that the competitor who first achieves three strikes is the victor.

There are no actual rounds at the open competitions. The match begins, and it continues until one of the competitors makes a point. The combatants are then recalled to the center of the ring, and the match is restarted. This continues until one of the competitors reaches the three-point level. He or she then becomes the winner.

Scoring in the open tournament is restricted to offensive maneuvers. These tournaments are considered light-contact events, though much harder contact is often witnessed. Punches and kicks are the primary tools of offense. No defensive maneuvers, such as intercepting an attack and throwing the opponent to the ground, are allowed.

The viable strike points at the open tournament are from the belt up. This includes the front and side of the body and head. No striking is allowed below the belt. If a combatant inadvertently turns around while sparring, no striking is allowed to the back, or the back of the head.

Once a competitor has won a match, he or she continues competing against other winning participants of the same belt and weight division. This process goes forward until the final match of a specific weight class takes place. Ultimately, one individual walks away as the victor.

At the end of the black-belt competition, the winning competitors fight one another. Many times there will be a 150-pound black belt competing against a 300-pound black belt, to decide the ultimate champion of the tournament. This is much different from Olympic-style taekwondo.

## Non-WTF Tournaments

Because the World Taekwondo Federation (WTF) and its sanctioned governing bodies are the sole source for taekwondo's inclusion into the Olympics, many non-WTF schools and organizations have no formalized focus for competition. To deal with this problem, many of these schools and organizations have begun to host taekwondo-oriented competitions that provide the non-WTF taekwondo practitioner with a place for competition. Some of these events, especially the ones hosted by the International Taekwondo Federation, tend to be very large occasions.

At these events, the structure is very similar to that of the open tournament. The primary difference is that the participants are made up entirely of taekwondo practitioners.

## Olympic-Style Taekwondo

The structure of Olympic-style taekwondo tournaments is highly formalized. They are very different from open tournaments and many of the tournaments hosted by non-WTF affiliate organizations.

Tournaments sponsored by WTF affiliate organizations are the breeding ground for tomorrow's Olympic athletes. As a result, these competitions are strictly structured and scrutinized. Every element of these tournaments, from the smallest detail to the larger visions, is presented with the rules and structure of Olympic-style taekwondo in mind. For example, in open tournaments, participants may wear whatever style of uniform they feel is appropriate. The Olympic-style taekwondo participant, on the other hand, is only allowed to wear the official WTF uniform.

There are two levels of taekwondo competition, the open tournament and the Olympic-style competition.

The official WTF uniform is made up of white pants and a white V-necked top with black trim. While protective gear is rarely seen in the open tournament, it is required in the world-class events. This equipment includes the body-protecting padded vest, the head protector, a groin guard, forearm guards, and shin guards.

The judging of the local, national, and international Olympic-style taekwondo events is also highly monitored. In the open tournament, any black belt can be a judge. This is not the case with Olympic-style taekwondo. All judges must be WTF-certified black belts (or black belts certified by a WTF-affiliated national organization) who have gone through an extensive training course. At the end of this course, they must pass a final exam in order to qualify to judge a competition.

Olympic-style taekwondo sparring competitions are fought in an eight-meter by eight-meter contest arena. Although this rule is not yet universally applied, the competitions are normally held on high-density foam rubber mats. The actual match consists of three three-minute rounds. Between the rounds, there is a one-minute period of rest.

Each match has four corner judges, who award points. For a point to be valid, it must be called by at least two of the judges.

There is also a referee who manages the match but does not award points. He can, however, award penalty points for violations of the rules, and in the case of a scoreless match he is the one who will decide the outcome, which is based on the technical superiority of one combatant over the other.

The techniques permitted in Olympic-style taekwondo tournaments are highly restricted. The permitted techniques are divided between punching and kicking offensive attacks.

The rules require punching techniques to use only the front part of a tightly clenched fist. Only punches to the torso are permitted, and punches are often not scored, as they are not considered a decisive enough technique. The permitted kicking techniques are made up of the various taekwondo kicks. These attacks may utilize any part of the foot, below the ankle. No knee attacks are allowed.

In open tournaments and non-WTF tournaments, the competitor who scores the first three points, or strikes, in the match is the winner, whereas in Olympic-style tournaments, the competitor who gains the most points within the three three-minute rounds emerges the victor.

The permitted areas of attack, in a sanctioned taekwondo match, are the torso and the face. The front and sides of the body are suitable attack areas. Appropriate attacks may be launched against any area of the torso covered by the vest protector. No attacks are allowed to the back of an opponent's torso. The face and sides of the head are also viable kicking targets. The back of the opponent's head may only be struck when a frontal assault has been unleashed, however.

# chapter 22
# competitive
# training

**P**REPARATION to enter a taekwondo sparring competition begins long before you ever take that step onto the competitive mat. It begins with your repetitive studio training, honing your punches and kicking skills, followed by your solo and partner training drills, your cardioaerobic conditioning training, and finally your long hours of sparring against other practitioners at your school. From this training you reach a point where you understand that to take the next step in your evolving mastery of taekwondo, you must face an unknown opponent.

## Your First Match

Entering your first sparring competition is an exhilarating experience. No doubt you will be nervous and have many questions about whom you will fight, how you will react, and whether or not you will emerge victorious from the competition.

From your studio training, you will surely have sparred with many of your classmates. Once you enter a tournament, however, you will be fighting against someone you have never met. As each instructor's training method has a slightly different focus, you can be sure that you will be encountering new techniques or new applications of techniques that you cannot expect or anticipate.

## The Competitive Mindset

Tournaments and sparring matches are competitions, so you must possess the desire to win before you enter into these events. It is very easy to tell which practitioners have a winning mindset and which do not, at the beginning of every match. Focused competitors have a oneness of purpose to all of their actions: as they enter the ring, as they bow to the referee and their opponent, and as they compete. From this oneness of purpose, many matches are won before they ever begin.

How do you develop a competitive mindset? Begin by being sure of what you are doing and why you are doing it.

If you are simply fighting because your instructor, your parents, your husband, your wife, or your friends told you that you should, you should not be competing. Whether you win or lose is irrelevant. You are not entering the event with a focused purpose.

> *C*ompetition is the best way to put your training to the test. You will be able to gauge your progress in taekwondo and learn which of your techniques are effective against an unknown opponent—and which of them need work.

Many people enter competition with a very casual mindset. This is not only bad for the sport but for all of the competitors.

If you do not possess the desire to take competition to the maximum level your body and mind will allow, then competition may not be for you. You can focus your training on taekwondo's many other aspects. If, on the other hand, you truly wish to test your skills against other competitors, and you see the experience—win or lose—as a way to make you a more complete individual and to strengthen your taekwondo skills, then you possess the correct motivation for entering competition.

# Training

You may have the desire to win a competition, but that does not mean you are going to win a tournament. Winning takes much more than simple desire. You must be willing to train your body harder than your opponent, and refine your skills to a greater degree. You must be willing to experience the pain associated with competition-level training, work through it, and continue toward your own path to victory.

## Devising a Competition Training Program

To compete in taekwondo competitions, not only must you have highly refined skills, but your cardiovascular endurance must be exceptionally high. To reach this level, you must devise an exacting training schedule that

It is essential to understand that your ability in a taekwondo sparring competition is directly related to the amount of effort you put into training. The more you train, the more you spar, the more you compete, the better you become.

hones both your taekwondo skills and your stamina.

Most world-class athletes begin their day with cardioaerobic exercise. This can be an extended run, a fast-paced bicycle ride, or a competitive swim.

As many athletes go to school or have a job, they spend much of their day attending to these necessities. After school is out or the job is over, training recommences.

For the taekwondo athlete, this will commonly mean going to the dojang and working out for several hours. During this period of training, at least one normal taekwondo class is attended each day. This focuses the competitor's training methodology and hones his or her basic skills. After the studio workout, the competitive taekwondo athlete will commonly return to a second form of cardioaerobic activity in the evening.

Although this may seem like an intense training schedule, there are many people around the world who do nothing but train all day long. These are the people you will encounter at taekwondo tournaments. If you wish to compete at their level, you must be willing to train as hard as you possibly can.

Certainly, if you are a weekend warrior, this level of intense training is not required and should not scare you away from your overall taekwondo training and your occasional foray into the taekwondo tournament. As each individual must find his or her own balance between personal life and taekwondo training, you can adjust your training schedule to meet your needs and your family's.

## Competitive Solo Training

When you arrive at your taekwondo studio for competitive training, you must be so focused that, if there are no other students in the school, you have a well thought out plan for your solo training. Simply going to your dojang and kicking the hanging bag for a few hours is never enough to enhance your competitive skills. You must enter with a single focus—that of improving your competitive skills.

In Part V of this book you were taught several techniques that are ideal for you to practice when you are training alone. As a competitor, however, you will want to raise the bar on those techniques and take your solo training to the next level.

It is assumed that at this point in your overall taekwondo development, you are physically fit to the point that you truly desire to put your body to the test. Therefore, you must not allow yourself to become lazy.

To begin, you will want to stretch and warm up. You will then want to run your body through the basic kicks. This will help you to focus your techniques.

When you have completed your basic exercises, your serious training begins—training that will help you in competition.

## Competitive Solo-Training Drill One

Competitive taekwondo requires you to unleash one technique after the next, so this drill is an ideal place to start your competitive solo training. Decide on a specific set of techniques—for example, a right-side front kick, followed by a left-side roundhouse kick, followed by a right-side roundhouse kick, followed by a left-side back kick, culminating with a right-side jumping back kick. Perform this series of kicks twenty times as quickly and precisely as possible. The moment you have completed your twentieth repetition, drop down and perform twenty push-ups.

Immediately upon the completion of the push-ups, jump up and unleash another series of twenty kicking techniques. This time, perhaps you will deliver a right-side axe kick, followed by a left-side axe kick, followed by a right-side spinning axe kick, culminating with a left-side spinning heel kick.

When you have completed this series, again drop to the ground and perform twenty push-ups. Upon arising, take a few minutes, catch your breath, and begin the process again.

Not only is this a great form of cardioaerobic exercise, but it will push your body to the limit. This gives you a chance to find out what kicking techniques you are the most proficient with, and can therefore rely on when your body is extended to the limit. These are the kicking techniques to resort to when you are in the middle of competition and are feeling drained.

## Competitive Solo-Training Drill Two

This is another ideal competitive solo-training drill to perform after your initial warmup. Stand in front of the studio hanging bag. Enter into a fighting stance. When you are ready, rapidly deliver twenty roundhouse kicks per leg, alternating your legs with each kick. Powerfully kick the bag with each technique.

The moment you have completed this kicking series, rapidly run in place for three minutes. When your three minutes are up, rapidly roundhouse kick the bag for a second series.

Performing this exercise for a series of five to ten full repetitions will not only hone your roundhouse kicking skills, an essential element of sparring, but will provide you with a cardioaerobic workout, as well. Therefore, this is an ideal competition-level, solo-training exercise.

### Competitive Solo-Training Drill Three

The back kick is an ideal defensive weapon. Most taekwondo practitioners never develop this kick for use in a defensive application, however. Therefore, you will want to develop the ability to unleash your back kick in an exclusively defensive manner.

To develop the back kick as a viable defensive tool, begin by standing in front of the studio mirror, or find a focal point on the wall. Enter into a fighting stance. When you are ready, rapidly retreat from your standing location, delivering alternating back kicks with each step.

Drive back as far as your training space allows. Once you have reached your end point, either turn around and perform the same kicking motion in the opposite direction, or run up to your original starting point and perform the exercise again, for a minimum of ten repetitions.

Initially, you may find this a bit difficult. As you develop this skill, however, it will become an essential tool in your defensive arsenal.

## Competitive Partner Training

At the heart of a competitive taekwondo practitioner's workout schedule is partner training. Just as partner training focuses the skills of the average taekwondo practitioner, it is even more important to the competitor. As such, a partner-training program must be laid out if you are planning to enter competitions.

As detailed in Part V of this book, an ideal method of partner training is focus glove practice. For this, your training partner will put on focus gloves, and you will kick toward them, thereby focusing your techniques and developing pinpoint accuracy.

To move this training up to the competitive level, you will want to turn up the speed. This will not only give you an essential understanding of your kicking arsenal, but it will force you to perform these techniques when you are winded.

**Competitive Partner-Training Drill One**

Face off with your training partner, who has a focus glove on each hand. Decide which single technique you are going to unleash. An ideal example is the roundhouse kick, as this kick is an essential element of victory in a taekwondo competition.

When you are both set, launch in at your training partner with one roundhouse kick after another—alternating legs with each kick. Your training partner will move back, causing you to move in, with each successive technique. If your partner backs up to the wall, he or she will immediately pivot and change direction, and you will continue forward with your roundhouse kick onslaught.

Training with a partner is essential if you're planning to enter competitions.

This kicking drill should be performed for a specific number of minutes, as opposed to a specific number of kicks. The ideal time frame is three minutes, as this is the length of a round in a taekwondo match.

This exercise, will force you to push yourself and your technique to the limit—just as you will be required to do in competition. In the early stages of this exercise, it is common for the practitioner to wish to stop. Do not let yourself. Force yourself to continue forward, even if your kicks begin to lack power. As time progresses, you will be able to last the duration without any hesitation.

**Competitive Partner-Training Drill Two**

Beyond simple cardioaerobic focus training, you will need to take partner training to the next step if you want to master the finer points of competition. This next step is simulated combat.

Although you must spar as much as possible if you wish to become a competitive taekwondo martial artist, sparring does not cause you to focus your training on specific aspects of your offensive and defensive capabilities. Therefore, partner drills have been designed to refine your taekwondo, to make you a more skillfully exact competitor.

To begin this competition-oriented partner-training drill, put your hands behind your back and hold one wrist with the other hand. Throughout this drill, you will not let your hands come forward.

Your hands are commonly used to balance your body. This is especially true when you are kicking. By removing your hands from the equation, you force yourself to learn a new method to balance your body. From this, you will gain new mastery of taekwondo.

Once you are both ready, launch into offensive attacks toward your training partner. Utilize whatever kicking technique you desire. Your partner can block in whatever manner he or she feels is most appropriate, but cannot counter-attack.

Continue this pattern for a three-minute round. Rest for one minute, as is stipulated by the rules of Olympic-style taekwondo, and then put your hands behind your back for your second round. In this round, your opponent will attack you. As you cannot defend yourself with the common blocking techniques, you must find a new method to get out of the path of an attack.

This is an ideal training exercise to take you to the next level of taekwondo mastery. From it, you will learn how to control your offense and defense in a nontraditional manner. This may well give you the advantage in a sparring competition.

# footwork

**F**OOTWORK, or *jitgi*, refers to your ability to place yourself where you want to be in the midst of competition, and to move yourself out of unfavorable locations. To the average individual, footwork is just a random set of occurrences that causes them to move in or move out of a particular situation. To the taekwondo practitioner, footwork is a science.

Footwork training is an essential element of your sparring education. It teaches you the best method to move in on an opponent and then strike with an appropriate offensive attack. With an understanding of footwork, you also know the best way to move out of the path of an attack, allowing you to defend yourself or immediately counterstrike.

## Linear Footwork

The first style of footwork employed in tae-kwondo is known as "linear footwork." Linear footwork is broken up into two categories: (1) forward footwork, which is known in Korean as *naga jitgi*, and (2) reverse footwork, which is known by the Korean term *mullo jitgi*.

### Forward Footwork

Training in forward footwork teaches you to rapidly move in toward your opponent and attack with one very direct linear movement. This forward motion can take the form of either a step or a slide. An ideal example of this occurs when a match begins and you immediately

**T**he word *jitgi* is the Korean term used to describe "footwork." The main styles of footwork are *naga jitgi*, which means "forward footwork"; *mullo jitgi*, which means "reverse footwork"; *bekyo jitgi*, which means "lateral footwork"; and *dwi dora jitgi*, which means "turning footwork."

slide in toward your opponent and deliver a front kick to his midsection, under his guard.

### Reverse Footwork

Training in reverse footwork teaches you to rapidly move back, away from the onslaught of an opponent, in a linear pattern. As in the case of forward footwork, this movement may take the form of a step or a slide. A jump back is also a possible type of reverse footwork.

The common reason for retreating in this fashion is that your opponent has launched an attack at you. Instead of blocking it, you wish to reposition yourself to launch a counterattack. An ideal example of this is seen in the case of an axe kick being launched in your direction. You slide back out of its path and then immediately counter with a roundhouse kick.

## Lateral Footwork

The next form of footwork you must master is the lateral move. When performing this technique, you move from side to side while in competition.

The basic application of lateral footwork, *bekyo jitgi*, is to simply slide or step to the side when a linear attack has been launched against you. This action is performed to allow you to reposition yourself for a counterstrike. For example, suppose your opponent has attempted a side kick. You would simply slide to one side, out of the path of the attack, and then immediately counterstrike him with a roundhouse kick or other appropriate technique.

At the more advanced level of lateral footwork, you pivot out of the path of an oncoming attack. For example, suppose a front kick is launched at you. Leaving your lead leg in place, you pivot backward on the ball of your foot, out of the path of the attack. Once the attack has missed, you immediately pivot back into position and launch a counterstrike.

## Turning Footwork

Turning footwork, *dwi dora jitgi*, is the most advanced level of footwork employed by the taekwondo practitioner. With turning footwork, you actually spin out of the path of an attack, continue with the spin, and launch your own offensive assault. For example, suppose your opponent attempts to kick you with an axe kick. You pivot out of the path of the attack on the ball of your foot.

You then continue spinning through, delivering a spinning heel kick to his head.

This level of footwork is only for the most advanced practitioners, who understand their own offensive speed and capabilities. In addition, they must understand the dynamics of their opponent, in order to set the opponent up for this level of counterattack.

## The Feint

A feint is a mock attack intended to distract the attention of your opponent. To use this type of footwork, you can simply rapidly jump forward and stamp your lead foot as it lands on the ground. This may well distract your opponent for a second. In this moment of indecision, you can launch a powerful secondary attack, such as a rear-leg front kick—thereby scoring a point.

> Taekwondo footwork is not solely designed to be utilized in defensive and counterstriking applications. It is also a means to lure your opponent into assuming that one type of attack is about to take place, when, in fact, you intend to launch something completely different.

## Developing Footwork

The development and application of footwork is a personal process for the taekwondo practitioner. It is something that is achieved through time and with extensive amounts of practice.

It is essential to understand that each opponent will deal with your footwork in his or her own unique manner. Therefore, the style of footwork that will cause you to emerge victorious from a match with one competitor may not work with another. For this reason, you must first develop an overall pattern of footwork technique that works with your body type and level of competition. You must then be willing to alter this pattern, to deal with the specific type of opponent you are fighting.

# chapter 24
# competitive
# strategy

ONCE YOU HAVE TRAINED to what you believe is an appropriate level, it is time for you to devise a strategic game plan for competition. Through your ongoing sparring training, you will have learned what works best for you—which techniques you can perform most accurately. On the basis of this inner knowledge, you will want to formalize a plan for entering a competition.

## The Four Rules of Competition

The four basic rules of competition are:

1. Do not attempt to use a technique you have not fully mastered.
2. Do not attempt to use fancy or overexaggerated techniques.
3. Do not hesitate.
4. Do not overexert yourself too early in a match.

## Do Not Attempt to Use a Technique You Have Not Fully Mastered

Use techniques that you can execute as precisely as possible, even if these techniques are some of the most basic. Many novice practitioners decide to experiment while competing. This is a mistake. A savvy opponent can easily see when a technique is being deployed in an inexpert or unbalanced way. He or she will instantly take advantage of your lack of control and quickly drive a powerful counterstriking technique home—thereby, scoring a point.

## Do Not Attempt to Use Fancy or Overexaggerated Techniques

Although taekwondo is full of very fancy, high-flying kicks—in which the practitioner jumps up in the air, spins around, and guides a kick toward its target—these elaborate kicks are only to be used in demonstrations and as training tools. Their exaggerated nature may make these techniques beautiful to watch, but they are very easy to defend against. If you attempt to use one of these kicks in competition, no matter how well you have developed your technique, a competent opponent will immediately move in on you and score an offensive point.

## Do Not Hesitate

The most common problem with losing competitors is that they hesitate. They do not immediately launch into an attack the moment a match has begun; throughout the match, they think and decide what they should do next.

Through training and sparring practice, you must reach a point where you simply react—you know what to do. Thinking and preparing a strategy of what to do next, while a match is under way, will only slow you down.

Practice in the studio. In competition, act and react, but do not hesitate.

## Do Not Overexert Yourself Too Early in a Match

A common offensive tactic is to rush into a match and unleash a great many offensive techniques. This is done in hopes of intimidating the opponent.

When you perform this tactic against a savvy competitor, he or she will simply allow you to wear yourself out. Although you may score a few initial points, most likely, you will not be able to keep up this pace in the second and third rounds. Expending an enormous amount of energy during the first round you will tire out too soon.

This is not a good fighting strategy. The seasoned opponent will simply wait you out and then score point after point in the later rounds. Therefore, it is essential to pace yourself throughout a sparring competition.

# Offensive or Defensive Methodology

Each taekwondo competitor must decide which sparring methodology he or she will use in each match—offensive or defensive. Some people are naturally

No one can tell you how to compete. Instructors and coaches will tell you what has worked for them, what you should try, and why you should try it. This is all a part of training. Ultimately, however, it is you who must decide your tactical method of operations for yourself. Only after extended sparring practice will you be ready to make this choice.

drawn to one or the other. Some practitioners are very aggressive by nature. Thus, they gravitate toward a very offensive approach to sparring. They want to get in there and hit. Others are more calculating and want to outsmart their opponents with counterstriking measures.

Each sparring match you enter is different. Each opponent you are matched up against competes in a different way. Obviously, you will need to tailor your chosen sparring style to meet the needs of each particular match, but, as a competitor, you must first formalize a plan of winning—an offensive or defensive methodology.

To do this, experiment with your offensive and defensive options while training. Come to a conclusion about which approach suits you best. From this, move forward into the world of competition with a definite game plan for using your finest skills and becoming the best competitor you can be.

# part 7
# advancing
# in taekwondo

**A**s a student of taekwondo, you have entered into a world where there is never an end point, never a stage at which you know all that you can know. You have entered a path of continued physical and mental evolution.

Through the art of taekwondo, you will continually refine your body and your mind, becoming more proficient with the physical techniques that make up this advanced system of self-defense, while gaining more understanding of body mechanics. At each stage of your life, you will be able to adapt your body to the physical techniques that are most suited to your age. Hand in hand with this, you will continue an ongoing process of developing a clearer understanding of the advanced subtleties of this art, while becoming more proficient at explaining and teaching taekwondo to the world.

# developing a training schedule

**A**S A NEW STUDENT of taekwondo, you will be very excited about the training you are experiencing and will want to train as much as possible. As many novice practitioners have discovered, however, this enthusiasm may fade.

There are any number of reasons why people lose their excitement about taekwondo training. It may be due to the stresses of school, work, or family. In some cases, people enter a taekwondo program expecting to become master fighters overnight. When they are defeated in a sparring competition by a younger opponent, who has trained for a longer period of time, they recognize the long road ahead of them, become disillusioned, and leave taekwondo behind. Other students, after a period of training, decide that there is nothing more they need to learn.

A competent taekwondo instructor understands all of these variables and can help dedicated students work through any questions and remain in training. But sometimes this is just not enough. Students will leave the program.

If you truly wish to maintain your focus on taekwondo, you will need to set up some standards by which you will train. Most important is to set up a training schedule that fits the needs of your life.

Of course, life events come up, and sometimes we must bow out of an activity on a particular day. If this happens to you, do not become upset, simply come back the next day and recommit yourself to your training schedule.

## Progressing in Taekwondo

Some people who begin training in taekwondo expect to become black-belt masters of the art overnight. Progress takes work. If you want to master the art of taekwondo, you must work at it. This is a key element that many people overlook.

If all you want is to own a black belt, many stores sell them. To be a true black belt, however, requires a long period of intense training. For this reason, it is essential to be realistic about your training program. Before you begin training at a school, ask what you can expect to learn at each level of your education. This will give you a realistic understanding of the course your taekwondo training will take, and how soon you can expect to progress between belts and levels of expertise.

> Many novice students would like to train seven days a week, but this is unrealistic for virtually anyone. Therefore, you must decide upon a realistic training schedule. Whether you commit to training one day or five days a week, once you have decided upon it, you must follow through.

## Burnout

Burnout is also a common occurrence among taekwondo students. Burnout happens for any number of reasons, and to all levels of taekwondo practitioners.

You can recognize burnout by the feeling that you just do not have the motivation or desire to train any longer. You simply no longer experience any benefit from taekwondo participation.

There are a couple of things you can do to work through burnout. First and perhaps most important, integrate a new style of training into your overall taekwondo regimen. This can mean adding a new form of cardioaerobic exercise to your training program, training with some new partners, or simply focusing your solo training on some new aspect of taekwondo that you really wish to master. All of these things can give you new enthusiasm for the art.

Another great way to overcome burnout is to begin teaching. Even if you are not at the assistant instructor level at your school, you can gather together some of your friends and teach them some of the basic techniques you have learned, or simply help the lower belts in your class. From teaching comes a great sense of accomplishment. This will help you to revitalize your enthusiasm for taekwondo.

Ultimately, to overcome burnout, you must make a conscious decision to stay active with taekwondo. Sometimes just making that mental commitment to keep training will get you through burnout and provide you with focus, until you find new motivation for taekwondo participation.

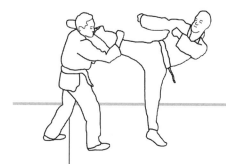

# promotion

**V**IRTUALLY EVERYONE who begins taekwondo training hopes to wear the black belt one day. Rising to the black-belt level is an ongoing process, however. It is essential to realize that the process of earning the black belt is even more important than actually obtaining it, for that is how the fundamentals of taekwondo are mastered.

## The Promotional Test

Each level of taekwondo training emphasizes the ongoing development of the practitioner's physical and mental capabilities. To assess a student's ongoing development in taekwondo, promotional tests are held throughout the year.

**P**romotional tests include:

☞ warmups

☞ blocking, punching, and kicking drills

☞ poomse

For more advanced students, tests also include:

☞ one- and three-step sparring

☞ board breaking

These tests are normally held every three months at most schools of taekwondo. Students who have attended class on a regular basis and shown progress in their understanding of the art are allowed to test for promotion to the next *gup* level, at each of these three-month intervals.

Taekwondo promotional tests are judged in one of two ways. If a school has a small student body, promotional tests are commonly judged solely by the instructor. If, on the other hand, a school has a large number of students, then the students are evaluated by a panel of black-belt judges.

Promotional tests commonly begin with a warmup, led by one of the senior students or assistant instructors. The students are then led

It is essential to remember that your instructor would not have told you that you were ready to test if you were not. So, keeping that in mind, simply do your best, and you will do fine.

through various blocking, punching, and kicking drills, either individually or in a group of the same rank. These drills demonstrate a student's ongoing development and proficiency in taekwondo's fundamental techniques. The students are then instructed, either individually or as a group, to perform the appropriate *poomse* for their belt division.

It is very common in a taekwondo promotional test to witness the higher belts performing all the testing requirements for the lower-belt divisions. As each gup level completes testing, they will sit down, leaving the higher belts remaining.

As a practitioner moves to the higher belts in taekwondo, he or she is expected to possess a higher level of physical fitness. Testing provides the judges with insight into the overall level of fitness and stamina possessed by an individual who is being evaluated for a higher rank.

Once the poomse segment of the test is complete, various other tests are performed. These segments vary from school to school, and are determined by the master instructor. Most commonly, the next phase of testing involves one-step sparring and three-step sparring. Once this segment is complete, many schools will have their students perform board-breaking techniques. The actual technique of the break will either be called out by the judges or will be predetermined by the school's testing procedure.

Once this part of the test is complete, sparring begins. Here, a student will be put up against another student of similar rank, and they will be judged on their offensive and defensive capabilities. For the high-rank testing, students are commonly asked to spar against two or more opponents, to test their timing and self-defense skills against multiple attacks.

## Preparing for a Test

Your first test can be a nerve-racking experience, but this is simply because you do not know what to expect. The testing procedure for each school follows a very specific pattern, however, so if you want to know what the test consists of, simply ask your instructor or an advanced student. They will be happy to tell you what to expect.

The best thing you can do to prepare for a promotional test is to simply work on the required blocks, punches, kicks, and poomse for your specific belt division, until you know them. Then, go to the test and do the best job you can.

## Testing Fee

Most schools of taekwondo charge a fee for promotional testing. This fee not only helps to keep the doors of the studio open, but also pays for the belt, if your belt color changes, and for a certificate of promotion, if your school offers them.

Common testing fees are from twenty-five to fifty dollars for the lower belts. At some schools the testing fee increases for each belt level you ascend to. It is a good idea to ask about this fee when you join a school, so it won't come as a surprise when it is time to test.

Black-belt testing fees tend to be very high at most schools of taekwondo. They range in price from $100 on up. Most first dan testing fees are in the $300 range. As one moves up through the black-belt dans, one can expect the testing fee to move up too. Again, these testing fees help to keep the studio in operation and pay for belts and certificates.

Unfortunately, some people are held back in rank by the testing fees. They possess the skills to advance, but they do not have the money. It is sad when a taekwondo practitioner's career is held back in this way, but it does not look as if these testing fees will decrease in the near future.

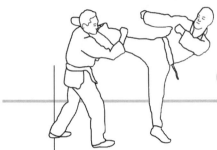

# chapter 27
# demonstrations

**D**EMONSTRATING your proficiency in taekwondo in front of spectators can be an exciting and exhilarating experience. It introduces your audience to this advanced system of self-defense and can bring many new students into your school.

Taekwondo demonstrations are held in many venues. These include martial arts tournaments, cultural festivals, high schools, universities, and any place where the audience may appreciate seeing taekwondo demonstrated in its most elaborate forms.

Whereas contestants in taekwondo sparring competitions must demonstrate their proficiency by battling against other practitioners, taekwondo martial artists who participate in a demonstration get to perform their best techniques without worrying about counterattacks.

## Elements of the Demonstration

Taekwondo demonstrations are commonly made up of three primary elements. There is the poomse demonstration, the self-defense demonstration, and the breaking demonstration. Of course, there are variations, but these are the basic components witnessed in a taekwondo demonstration.

**D**emonstrations are usually made up of three parts

☞ poomse demonstrations

☞ self-defense demonstrations

☞ breaking demonstrations

### The Forms Segment

The poomse, or forms, segment of a taekwondo demonstration usually consists of the various belt groupings performing their appropriate forms in unison. You will commonly see all of the yellow-belt members of a school organize in a formation, then the command to begin will be called, and the students will perform their poomse. This initial yellow-belt segment may immediately be followed by the blue belts, the red belts, and so on.

The reason novice yellow belts and then intermediate blue belts are allowed to perform in demonstrations is that it gives the audience an idea of the degree of technical skill that goes hand in hand with each level of taekwondo training. This shows any potential students what they can expect to learn and when they will learn it, if they begin taekwondo training.

It is not uncommon, at the black-belt level, to see very elaborate variations on the traditional forms. Here, one commonly witnesses advanced spinning and jumping kicks being integrated into the poomse, to show the audience what an advanced system of kicking taekwondo possesses.

### The Self-Defense Segment

The next segment of a taekwondo demonstration commonly involves various self-defense applications.

In a school of taekwondo, the self-defense training is very realistic. In a demonstration, this is not necessarily the case. In this segment, you will see taekwondo practitioners acting out various scenarios, and perhaps flying through the air when they are struck by a kick. Although all of the techniques are obviously based on taekwondo, this segment is more on par with movie choreography than with the implementation of actual fighting skills.

This segment is designed not only to entertain the viewers, but to give them an idea of the vast array of techniques that the art of taekwondo can teach. Again, this has the potential to draw new students into a school.

### The Breaking Segment

In the breaking segment of a taekwondo demonstration, the audience will commonly see taekwondo practitioners breaking boards or bricks with various punching or kicking techniques. This demonstrates the power of taekwondo and allows the audience to appreciate the discipline that goes into the study of this art, in order to master these impressive techniques.

## Preparing for a Demonstration

As a student of taekwondo, you may well be asked to take part in a demonstration that your school is hosting. This may make you nervous at first, but remember that you will only be performing techniques that your instructor knows you have mastered—so, relax.

To prepare for the demonstration, simply practice your routine as much as possible. If you are going to perform a form, practice it until it becomes second nature. If you are going to demonstrate self-defense applications, practice with your partner until you are both 100 percent comfortable with the process. Then, agree that if either of you forgets a part of the routine, you will not stop and signal your mistake, but simply go on with another technique, as if nothing has gone wrong. If you are going to perform a break, keep yourself focused, and do not become distracted by the crowd. Aim at your target and punch or kick through it.

With practice, any demonstration can go off without any problems. Preparing for a demonstration is, in fact, a great way for you to perfect elements of your taekwondo. This is because you will need to go through an incredible number of repetitive rehearsals that will make you focus your techniques to a degree never required in your normal taekwondo class. With a precisely orchestrated program and refined personal skills, you will be able to show your love for taekwondo to the world.

# Taekwondo Organizations

AAU Taekwondo National
Headquarters
The Walt Disney World Resort
P.O. Box 10,000
Lake Buena Vista, FL 32830
Tel: 407-934-7200
Tel: 518-372-6849
Fax: 407-934-7242
www.aautaekwondo.org

African Taekwondo Union
10 East Road, Avondale
Harare, Zimbabwe
Tel: 263-4-733405
Tel: 263-91-223889
Fax: 263-4-732430

American Taekwon-do Federation
1423 18th Street
Bettendorf, IA 52722
Tel: 563-359-7000
Fax: 563-355-7299

Asian Taekwondo Union
1211, Life Officetel
61-3, Euido-dong,

Youngdeongpo-gu,
Seoul, South Korea 150-731
Tel: 82-2-780-0707
Fax: 82-2-780-0708

Association Suisse de Taekwondo
Hohenstrasse 45
CH2562 port, Switzerland
Tel: 41-32-331-1151
Fax: 41-32-331-2151
www.taekwondo.ch

Belgian National Taekwondo Union
77 Avenue Broustin
1083 Bruxelles, Belgium
Tel: 32-2-426-54-68
Fax: 32-2-426-54-23

British Taekwondo Control Board
11 Hassocks Hedge, Banbury Lane
Northampton NN4 9QA,
United Kingdom
Tel: 44-1604-460800
Fax: 44-1604-460800
www.btcb.org

British United Taekwon-Do
Federation
58 Wiltshire Lane
Eastcote, Pinner
Middlesex HA5-2LU,
United Kingdom
Tel: 44-0181-429-0878

Cambodian Taekwondo Federation
B.P. 101
Olympic National Complex
Sportive Stadium
Phnom Penh, Cambodia
Tel: 855-23-215659
Tel: 855-12-804740
Tel: 855-11-839869
Fax: 855-23-364752
Fax: 855-23-215659

Chinese Taipei Amateur
Taekwondo Association
No 456, 5th Floor, Chungshan N.
Rd.
Sector 6
Taipei, Taiwan
Tel: 886-2-2872
Tel: 886-2-0780
Tel: 886-2-0781
Fax: 886-2-2873
Fax: 886-2-2246

Confederation Argentina de
Taekwondo
Scalabrini Ortiz Piso 6
Buenos Aires CP 1414, Argentina
Tel: 54-11-4772
Tel: 54-11-6799

Tel: 54-11-4254
Tel: 54-11-2878
Fax: 54-11-4772, Fax: 54-11-6799

Confederação Brasileira de
Taekwondo
Palácios dos esportes
Rua Visconde de Inhauma
No. 39 sala 601
Centro Rio de Janeiro
RJ, Cep.20.091-007, Brazil
Tel: 55-21-233-4083
Tel: 55-21-537-4263
Fax: 55-21-233-3982

Cuba Taekwondo Federation
Calle 13, Esq,
C#601, Vedado
La Habana, Cuba
Tel: 537-408819
Tel: 537-402921
Tel: 537-417472
Fax: 537-335310
Fax: 537-669796

Deutsche Taekwondo Union
Luisenstrasse 3, 90762
Furth, Germany
Tel: 49-911-974-8888
Fax: 49-911-974-8890
www.dtu.de

Egyptian Taekwondo Federation
64 Ramsis Extention St.
Nasr City, Cairo, Egypt
Tel: 20-2-263-1737
Fax: 20-2-261-7576

European Taekwondo Union
267 Imittou Avenue
P.C.116.31
Pagrati, Greece
Tel: 3010-7565647
Tel: 3010-7565648
Tel: 3010-7565617
www.etutaekwondo.org

Federación de Taekwondo de
Puerto Rico
Calle Marginal #3
Ofio 2-B, Urub.
San Agustin, Rio Piedras,
Puerto Rico 00923
Tel: 1-787-274-1961
Tel: 1-787-748-2789
Fax: 1-787-274-1961

Federación Española de Taekwondo
Ondarroa, No. 8 Bajo
48004 Bilbao, Spain
Tel: 34-94-459-7068
Fax: 34-94-412-3548

Fédération Française de Taekwondo et Disciplines Associées
25 rue Saint Antoine
69003 Lyon, France
Tel: 33-437-561414
Fax: 33-437-561415
www.fftda.fr

Federación Mexicana de Taekwondo
Calle Incas No 12, Altos 29
Entre Peru Y Hondurasalena
Mixhuca

Col. Centro, CP06010, Mexico
Tel: 52-5-519-0113
Tel: 52-5-519-1279
Fax: 52-5-526-2830

Federação Portuguesa de
Taekwondo
Rua dos Correeiros,
221-2. Esq.
1100-165 Lisboa, Portugal
Tel: 351-21-324-0211
Fax: 351-21-324-0300
www.fpt.pt/federacao.php

Federazióne Italiana Taekwondo
Viale Tiziano 70
00196 Rome, Italy
Tel: 39-6-3685-8742
Tel: 39-6-3685-8740
Fax: 39-6-323-3673
www.taekwondowtf.it

Hapkido Taekwondo International
P.O. Box 500
Redondo Beach, CA 90277
Tel: 310-353-4517
www.hapkido-taekwondo.com

Hong Kong Taekwondo Association
Room 2012, Sport House
1 Stadium Path, So Kon Po
Causeway Bay, Hong Kong, China
Tel: 852-2504-8116
Tel: 852-2504-8117
Fax: 852-2881-0871

Indonesian Taekwondo Association
Kantor Induk-Induk Organisasi
Olahraga
Anggota Koni Pusat
Pintu I Stadium Utama Senayan
Jakarta Pusat, Indonesia
Tel: 62-21-573-5035
Fax: 62-21-573-5035

International TaeKwon-Do
Association
P.O. Box 281
Grand Blanc, MI 48439
Tel: 810-232-6482
Fax: 810-235-8594
www.itatkd.com

International Taekwon-Do
Federation
Drau Gasse 3
A-1210 Vienna, Austria
Tel: 292-8475; Tel: 292-5509
www.itf-taekwondo.com

Irish Taekwondo Union
14 Clontarf Road
Dublin 3, Republic of Ireland
Tel: 353-1-833-4453
Fax: 353-1-833-4453

Israel Taekwondo Federation
P.O.Box 7657
Jerusalem 91075, Israel
Tel: 972-2-678-0175
Fax: 972-2-624-3061

Japan Taekwondo Federation
Office 12F
2-6-4 Shinjuku
Shinjuku-ku, Tokyo 160-0022,
Japan
Tel: 81-3-3350-0500
Fax: 81-3-3350-0576

KoreAmerica TaeKwon-Do Union
441 South Main St., #97
Manchester, CT 06040
Tel: 860-649-9696
Fax: 860-649-1231
www.itf-katu.com

Korea Taekwondo Association
A-3, 88-2, Oryoon-Dong
Songpa-Gu, Seoul 138-151, Korea
Tel: 82-2-420-4271
Tel: 82-2-420-4272
Tel: 82-2-420-4273
Fax: 82 2 420 4274
www.koreataekwondo.org

Kukkiwon
World Taekwondo Headquarters
635, Yuksam-dong
Kangnam-gu
Seoul 135-080, Korea
Tel: 82-2-567-1058
Tel: 82-2-567-1059
Tel: 82-2-567-3024
Fax: 82-2-553-4728
www.kukkiwon.or.kr

Malaysia Taekwondo Association
First floor, Wisma O.C.M, Jalan
Hang Jebat
50150 Kuala Lumpur, Malaysia
Tel: 60-3-238-5041
Tel: 60-3-238-5494
Fax: 60-3-238-5055

Myanmar Taekwondo Federation
Aungsan Memorial Stadium
Mingala
Taungnyant Townships
P.O. Box 11221
Yangon, Myanmar
Tel: 951-274502
Tel: 951-282709
Fax: 951-571061
Fax: 951-277907

Nepal Taekwondo Association
P.O. Box 4933
Dasarath Rangashala, Tripureshwor
Kathmandu, Nepal
Tel: 977-1-473989
Tel: 977-1-262180
Fax: 977-1-474335
Fax: 977-1-371103

New Zealand Taekwondo
Federation
P.O. Box 14-540
Panmure, Auckland, New Zealand
Tel: 64-9-570-9228
Fax: 64-9-570-4311
www.nztf.org.nz

Pakistan Taekwondo Federation
59 Brito Road
G.P.O. Box 1222
Karachi-74800, Pakistan
Tel: 92-21-549710
Tel: 92-21-549310
Fax: 92-21-5897567

Pan American Taekwondo Union
440 S. Washington St.
Falls Church, VA 22046
Tel: 703-534-3737
Fax: 703-536-3223
www.patu.org

Philippine Taekwondo Association
Rizal Memorial Sports Complex
Pabio Ocampo Sr. St, Malate
P.O. Box 2272
Manila, Philippines
Tel: 63-2-522-0519
Tel: 63-2-524-0457
Tel: 63-2-522 5405
Tel: 63-2-844 2431
Fax: 63-2-522-0518
Fax: 63-2-844-7485
www.philippinetaekwondo.com

Russian Taekwondo Union
8 Luzhnetskaya nab
Moscow 119871, Russia
Tel: 07-95-201-0628
Fax: 07-095-725-4708

Singapore Taekwondo Federation
3 Queens Road, #04-167
Singapore 1026

Tel: 65-345-1491
Fax: 65-459-3389

South African Taekwondo
Federation
P.O. Box 1355
Houghton 2041
Republic of South Africa
Tel: 27-11-403-3788
Tel: 27-082-990-3592
Fax 27-11-483-2726

Sri Lanka Taekwondo Federation
Grand Stand, 7A, Reid Avenue
Colombo-7, Sri Lanka
Tel: 94-1-689538
Fax: 94-1-689588

Taekwondo Association of China
9 Tiyuguan Road
Beijing 100763
People's Republic of China
Tel: 86-10-6702-1299
Tel: 86-10-6702-0345
Fax: 86-10-6702-0296

Taekwondo Association of Thailand
Room 239, West Zone
Rajamangala National Stadium
Sport Authority of Thailand
2088 Ramkhamhaeng Road, Huua-
mark, Bangkapi
Bangkok 10240, Thailand
Tel: 66-2-369-1518
Fax: 66-2-374-4653

Taekwondo Australia Inc.
24 Orion St.
Vermont, Melbourne VIC 3133,
Australia
Tel: 61-3-9874-7094
Fax: 61-3-9872-3747
www.taekwondoaustralia.org.au

Taekwondo Bond Nederland
P.O. Box 1490
NL-6501, BL Nijmegen,
The Netherlands
Tel: 31-24-323-9825
Fax: 31-24-360-3964
www.taekwondobond.nl

Taekwondo Federation of India
No 38, Chowdeshwari Temple
Street
Bangalore, 560 002, India
Tel: 91-80-221-2857
Fax: 91-80-221-9378
www.tfiindia.com

United States Taekwondo
Association
220 East 86th Street
New York, NY 10028
Tel: 212-772-8919
Fax: 212-772-3700

United States Taekwon-do
Federation
6801 W. 117th Ave., #E-5
Broomfield, CO 80020
Tel: 303-466-4963

United States Taekwondo Union
One Olympic Plaza, Suite 405
Colorado Springs, CO 80909
Tel: 719-866-4632
Fax: 719-866-4642
www.ustu.com

United States Taekwondo Won
9723 Kenwood Road
Cincinnati, OH 45242
Tel: 513-791-8888
Fax: 513-793-1803
www.ustw.org

Vietnam Taekwondo Association
4 Le Dai Hanh Street
District 11
Hochiminh City, Vietnam
Tel: 84-8-9623324
Fax: 84-8-9627472

WTF Taekwondo Association of
Canada
1300 Carling Avenue, Suite 208
Ottawa, Ontario, Canada K1Z 7L2
Tel: 613-792-3259
Fax: 613-792-3234
www.wtfcanada.com

# Books

Cho, Hee Il. *The Complete Tae Geuk and Black Belt Hyung*. W.T.F. Burbank, Calif.: Unique Publications, 2000.

——. *The Complete Tae Kwon Do Hyung* Vol. 1. Burbank, Calif.: Unique Publications, 1989.

——. *The Complete Tae Kwon Do Hyung* Vol. 2. Burbank, Calif.: Unique Publications, 1989.

——. *The Complete Tae Kwon Do Hyung* Vol. 3. Burbank, Calif.: Unique Publications, 1989.

Cho, Sihak Henry. *Tae Kwon Do: Secrets of Korean Karate*. Rutland: Charles E. Tuttle Co., Vt.: 1992.

Choi, Hong Hi. *Taekwondo*. Ontario: International Taekwondo Federation, 1972.

——. *Encyclopedia of Taekwondo*. 15 volumes, Geneva: International Taekwondo Federation, 2000.

Chun, Richard. *Advancing in Tae Kwon Do*. New York: HarperCollins, 1983.

——. *Moo Duk Kwan Tae Kwon Do: Korean Art of Self-Defense*. Valencia, Calif.: Black Belt Communications, Inc., 1975.

——. *Taekwondo: Spirit and Practice Beyond Self-Defense*. Jamaica Plain, Mass.: YMAA Publications, 2002.

——. *Tae Kwon Do: The Korean Martial Art*. New York: HarperCollins, 1976.

Eden, Karen and Keith D. Yates. *The Complete Idiot's Guide to Tae Kwon Do*. Indianapolis, Ind.: Alpha Books, 1998.

Gwon, Pu Gill. *Taegeuk: The New Forms of Tae Kwon Do*. Burbank, Calif.: Ohara Publications, 1980.

Kim, Sang H. *Taekwondo Kyorugi: Olympic Style Sparring*. Wethersfield, Conn.: Turtle Press, 1999.

Lee, Kyong Myong. *Dynamic Taekwondo: A Martial Art and Olympic Sport*. Warsaw: Hollym International Corporation, 1997.

Lee, Soon Man. *Modern Taekwondo: The Official Training Manual*. London: Sterling Publications, 1999.

Little, John R. and Curtis F. Wong, Eds. *Ultimate Guide to Tae Kwon Do*. Chicago: McGraw-Hill/Contemporary Books, 1999.

Park, Yeon Hee. *Tae Kwon Do: The Ultimate Reference Guide to the World's Most Popular Martial Art*. New York: Checkmark Books, 1999.

Rhee, Jhoon. *Chon-Ji of Tae Kwon Do-Hyung*. Valencia, Calif.: Black Belt Communications, Inc., 1989.

———. *Chung-Gun and Toi Gye of Tae Kwon Do Hyung*. Valencia, Calif.: Black Belt Communications, Inc., 1989.

———. *Hwa-Rang and Chung-Mu of Tae Kwon Do Hyung*. Valencia, Calif.: Black Belt Communications, Inc., 1989.

———. *Tan-Gun and To-San of Tae Kwon Do Hyung*. Valencia, Calif.: Black Belt Communications, Inc., 1989.

———. *Won-Hyo and Yul-Kok of Tae Kwon Do Hyung*. Valencia, Calif.: Black Belt Communications, Inc., 1989.

# Videos

Cho, Hee Il. *Tae Kwon Do Hyung* (1–10). Albuquerque, NM: Action International Martial Arts Association.

——. *Tae Kwon Do Hyung* (11–20). Albuquerque, NM: Action International Martial Arts Association.

——. *One Step and Three Step Sparring*. Albuquerque, NM: Action International Martial Arts Association.

——. *Taekwondo Basics: Techniques and Stances*. Albuquerque, NM: Action International Martial Arts Association.

Chun, Richard. *Taekwondo* Part 1. New York, NY: United States Taekwondo Association.

——. *Taekwondo* Part 2. New York, NY: United States Taekwondo Association.

Hee, Dana. *Taekwondo: Fighting Strategies for Modern Competition Sparring*. Burbank, Calif.: Unique Publications.

——. *Taekwondo: The ABC's of Modern Competition Sparring*. Burbank, Calif.: Unique Publications.

——. *Taekwondo: Training Drills for Modern Competition Sparring*. Burbank, Calif.: Unique Publications.

——. *Taekwondo: Sparring Strategies: For the Ring and the Street*. Burbank, Calif.: Unique Publications.

Kim, Sang H. *Beginner Taekwondo*. Wethersfield, Conn.: Turtle Press.

——. *Taekwondo Kicking Fundamentals*. Wethersfield, Conn.: Turtle Press.

——. *World Taekwondo Federation Black Belt Poomse*. Wethersfield, Conn.: Turtle Press.

——. *World Taekwondo Federation Palgwe Poomse*. Wethersfield, Conn.: Turtle Press.

——. *World Taekwondo Federation Taegeuk Poomse*. Wethersfield, Conn.: Turtle Press.

Perez, Herb. *Taekwondo: Advanced Sparring Techniques* Vols. 1–5. Valencia, Calif.: Black Belt Communications, Inc.

Reyes, Ernie. *Taekwondo* Vols. 1–5. Valencia, Calif.: Black Belt Communications, Inc.

# Periodicals

*Australian Taekwondo Magazine*
Blitz Publications
P.O. Box 4075
Mulgrave, Victoria
3170, Australia
Tel: 03-9574-8999
Fax: 03-9574-8899

*Black Belt Magazine*
Black Belt Communications
249 Anza Dr.
Valencia, CA. 91355
Tel: 661-257-4066

*Martial Arts*
CFW Enterprises, Inc.
4201 Vanowen Place
Burbank, CA 91505
Tel: 800-332-3330
Tel: 818-845-2656
Fax: 800-249-7761

Fax: 818-845-7761
www.cfwenterprises.com

*Taekwondo Choc Magazine*
Taekwondo Choc
Regie par la loi 1901
270/288 avenue de Pessicart/bât
F/les jardins de Babylone
06100 NICE
Tel: 33-04-9351-1212
Fax: 33-04-9351-1010
www.taekwondochoc.com

*Taekwondo Times*
Tri-Mount Publications
1423 18th Street
Bettendorf, IA 52722
Tel: 563-359-7202
Fax: 563-355-7299
www.taekwondotimes.com